2012

AND BEYOND

Also by Diana Cooper

Prepare for 2012 and Beyond
Double-CD (with Rosemary Stephenson)
Enlightenment through Orbs (with Kathy Crosswell)
Ascension through Orbs (with Kathy Crosswell)
Ascension through Orbs Meditations Double-CD
(with Kathy Crosswell)
The Orbs Cards (with Kathy Crosswell)
The Wonder of Unicorns
Unicorn Cards
A New Light on Angels
A New Light on Ascension
A Little Light on the Spiritual Laws
The Wisdom Cards (with Greg Suart)
Angel Answers
Angel Inspiration
Angels of Light Cards (2nd edition)
Angels of Light Cards Pocket Edition
Angels of Light Double-CD
Angels of Light Address Book
Angel Cards for Children
Teen-Angel (cards)
Angel Colouring Book
Discover Atlantis (with Shaaron Hutton)
The Atlantis Cards
Light Up Your Life

available from your local bookstore
or directly from publisher at
www.findhornpress.com

2012

AND BEYOND

DIANA COOPER

FINDHORN PRESS

© Diana Cooper 2009

The right of Diana Cooper to be identified as the author
of this work has been asserted by her in accordance with
the Copyright, Designs and Patents Act 1998.

ISBN 978-1-84409-182-9

Edited by Sabine Weeke and Carol Shaw
Proofread by Shari Mueller
Cover, interior design and illustrations by Damian Keenan
Printed and bound in the European Union

4 5 6 7 8 9 10 11 12 14 13 12 11 10

Published by
Findhorn Press
117-121 High Street,
Forres IV36 1AB,
Scotland, UK

t +44 (0)1309 690582
f +44 (0)131 777 2711
e info@findhornpress.com
www.findhornpress.com

2012

AND BEYOND

Diana Cooper

FINDHORN PRESS

Contents

Contents

Thanks

With thanks to Eckhard Graf, my German publisher, for persuading me to write this book and to Thierry Bogliolo and Sabine Weeke of Findhorn Press for their unfailing support. Also to Kathy Crosswell who has constantly encouraged me and helped me to fine-tune my connection to the angelic kingdom.

Words cannot express my gratitude to my guide Kumeka and to Metatron who have both stayed with me throughout. They are hard taskmasters but they never judge! Thanks also to the elemental kingdom that has also been with me during this time.

A small body of determined spirits
fired by an unquenchable
faith in their mission
can alter the course of history.

GANDHI

Introduction

I hope this book will give you information on more than the predictions based on current consciousness about the climatic, economic and political changes worldwide – more than information about the spiritual changes that will occur as portals open and massive new energies come in – more than the keys to switch on your own enlightenment and ascension. I believe this book will offer you courage and inspiration to move through the cleansing of the planet and the transformation in planetary consciousness to co-create the new Golden Age starting in 2032.

This book had quite a different birth from my other books. For the first time in years I was enjoying a few months without writing a book. I was really thinking I could get used to it! And my spiritual growth was accelerating rapidly as I spent hours quietly in the garden.

Then I received an e-mail from Eckhard Graf, my German publisher, asking me, please would I write a book on 2012 and beyond. As I had already produced some CD's on the subject Eckhard already knew it was my area. I felt such a surge of excitement that I knew I must do it. I was already planning the book in my head by the time I had finished reading the e-mail. In fact, I had written several chapters before I responded to him.

My guide, Kumeka, and Archangel Metatron, both of whom I work with said they would provide me with all the information I needed. As it happened, they later told me to also talk to the elementals in the garden and let them download information to me too. I have several fifth-dimensional elementals living in the trees at the end of my plot as well as hundreds of fairies, so I tried to balance my days by spending a few hours with my vegetables and some time writing each day.

Whilst I was completing this book I earned Metatron's gold and orange cloak and felt thrilled with this huge honour. He also gave me a symbol that I can use to attune to him more clearly. Now that I have received this cloak I can pass it on by harmonic transference to those who are ready. As Metatron is in charge of the thrust towards ascension taking place on Earth, this will accelerate your progress. If you accept it as you read these pages you can in turn pass it on to others. There are more details about this in the chapter on Metatron.

Last year I wrote *Enlightenment Through Orbs* and *Ascension Through Orbs* with Kathy Crosswell and communicated with her guide Wywyvsil. He is a Power (one of the highest frequency angels), a Lord of Karma, the Angel of Birth and runs many training schools on the inner planes, altogether a mighty being. When I started on this new book, Wywyvsil came forward and said that I was to link with him in the angelic realms, the seventh heaven, to bring that energy into the book, so that readers could unconsciously tune into the seventh dimension. That felt awesome!

2012 and beyond is such an important subject. We can follow the collective unconscious into doom and gloom or look at the amazing opportunities for soul growth and expansion that will be available. The changes outlined are almost unbelievably rapid and extraordinary. The spiritual energies coming in during 2012 are amazing and the world will be a very different place by 2032 as we receive back the wisdom from Golden Atlantis.

One evening as I was talking to a friend, Archangel Gabriel came in, feeling very serious. He told us that we must stop thinking about the past or worrying about the future. We humans are receiving special energies, which were sent thousands of years ago from the planets, particularly for this time. The messages they contain were formulated for us now because they knew then exactly what we would be going through.

Each day is now. In 2012 there will be a different now with another energy.

Archangel Gabriel said we of this planet are too tied up in what we are doing to pick up those dispatches that were sent with love and intention for us today. He reiterated, there is no other day, just now.

He continued that the directions are very clear. When we say the energy is high or low, we are only saying this because we are not tuning in and listening to the messages, which came from Source at the beginning of Creation.

Archangel Gabriel asks that you sit quietly for a little while each day. Open your heart to everything – the stars, animals, everything. Welcome and celebrate the energy every moment of the day and it will work with you.

SECTION 1

The Year 2012

CHAPTER 1

Ancient Prophecies
for 2012

THE 21ST DECEMBER 2012 *signifies the end of a 26,000-year astronomical period as well as a 260,000-year one. For the first time in the history of our planet, we are undertaking a double transformational leap. The possibilities for spiritual growth are enormous which is why nearly seven billion spirits have been allowed to incarnate for this monumental opportunity. And all the universes, without exception, are watching our progress with wonder and awe.*

~ The 260,000-Year Period Ending
21st December 2012 ~

This marks the end of the Atlantean era. The experiment of Atlantis was set up 260,000 years ago. It took 10,000 years to plan and prepare and lasted for 240,000 years. Although the landmass collapsed 10,000 years ago we are still within its influence until the end of 2012.

The aim of Atlantis was to see if humans could maintain a physical body, enjoy free will and still keep their connection with Source. There were many other humans who lived on other continents during that period but they were not part of that particular design. The final and fifth 10,000-year Atlantean period was a controlled experiment and during this time the Golden Age of Atlantis arose and lasted for 1,500 years. This period is the subject of my book *Discover Atlantis*. The divine vision is to bring back the energy of Golden Atlantis at an even higher level after 2032, this time for the whole world.

~ The 26,000-Year Period Ending
21st December 2012 ~

21st December 2012 also signifies the end of a 26,000-year astronomical period and the beginning of a new one. There will be a rare alignment between the earth and the sun on that day. In the past, when such an alignment occurred, because of the low consciousness of humanity, calamities and catastrophes followed. However this time we have an opportunity to create a different and glorious new age – but we are all asked to do our part, for the outcome is not yet assured.

Lady Gaia, the vast Being in charge of Earth, has decreed that Earth and all on her must ascend. That means everyone and everything has to rise in frequency. If we are ready, 2012 could be the start of a wonderful new way of living for all of us.

~ The 20-Year Transition
to the Golden Age ~

21st December 2012 marks the start of a new 20-year transition period that takes us to 2032. Then the new Golden Age truly begins.

On the winter solstice of 2012 Neptune, Pluto and Uranus are configured to interact. Neptune represents higher spirituality, Pluto transformation and Uranus change. As the energies work together, they will cause a massive impact on the consciousness of the planet. There is potential for a huge shift in frequency – individually and collectively – as long as we use the energy wisely.

The scheduled change is so enormous that the ancient wise ones could not predict what would happen beyond that date.

~ The Forecasts of the Ancients ~

THE MAYANS called 21st December 2012 'Creation Day', with a prophecy that the energy coming in on that day will activate the kundalini force in individuals and on the planet. The prophecies say that it will stimulate the genetic memories of our past lives and who we truly are and accelerate many into enlightenment and ascension.

They also project that the force of the planetary kundalini will help to activate and realign all the pyramids, which link us to our rightful place in the universe and that this will result in a rebirth of solar consciousness in humanity. The pyramids – Mayan, Egyptian and others – are cosmic computers. They are also generators and sub-stations for universal energy.

THE INCAS claim that before 2013 an asteroid will activate the purification of Earth.

THE AZTECS say that the current sun or 'ages' of the world is the fifth one, the end of a 26,000-year period.

Many of the **NATIVE AMERICAN** Wise Ones agree that the fifth world starts in 2012.

THE HOPI declare that 2012 is the end of an era – that after a 25-year period of purification there will be what they call 'The Emergence'.

THE CHEROKEE have their own calendar, which ends in 2012. They agree that previous worlds ended in cataclysms and it is possible that this one will too.

THE SENECA INDIANS say there will be a 25-year period of purification up to 2012.

THE MAORI tradition claims that there will be a lifting of the veils of illusion in 2012 and a merging of the physical and spiritual planes.

AFRICAN SHAMANS talk of 2012. The Zulus for example have a tale of cataclysm in 2012.

THE EGYPTIAN myths indicate that the end of 2012 heralds a planetary shift in consciousness.

THE GREAT CALENDAR OF THE PLEIADES, which is a cosmic calendar based on the movement of the Pleiades, ends on the 21st December 2012. Currently higher energies coming to Earth from other galaxies are stepped down through the Pleiades. At present many star children remain for a time on the Pleiades, a staging post before incarnation, in order to prepare for the slower frequencies on Earth. After 2012 all such star people will come directly into a physical incarnation without a transformer, and so will carry a higher vibration. They will have to choose a high frequency mother who can accommodate this.

THE TIBETAN AND JEWISH CALENDARS indicate that 2012 is the end of long cycle.

The Vedas declare that the ascent back to the light starts in 2012. Many **HINDUS** believe that Kalki, considered to be an avatar and the last incarnation of Lord Vishnu, will be fully realized by 2012. If he can enlighten 60,000 people before the winter solstice he can start a wave of enlightenment. If not, we on Earth will miss this extraordinary opportunity.

THE OUTBREATH OF BRAHMA is considered to last 26,000 years. At the end of the outbreath there is a cosmic moment, during which the portals of heaven open. In that silent moment miraculous things can happen, including a transformational leap for humankind.

EXERCISE: *Visualization to call in the Wise Elders*

1. Find a place where you can be quiet and undisturbed.
2. If you can, light a candle or play gentle, relaxing music
3. Take a few moments to breathe yourself into a comfortably relaxed space.
4. Visualize yourself sitting under an ancient tree as the sun is setting.
5. Call in the wise elders from different cultures. Honour them as they arrive.
6. Ask questions or listen to them communicating with each other.
7. Feel the energy of their wisdom and deep connection with the planet.
8. Know that non-linear time has passed as you watch the sun beginning to rise on a new day.
9. Thank the elders as they leave your space.
10. Open your eyes knowing that the new is starting for you.

CHAPTER 2

The 25-Year Period of Purification

Nearly all the wise ancients included in their prophecies the fact that a twenty-five-year period of purification would take place before 2012. Quetzalcoatl made a prophecy called the 13 Heavens and 9 Hells. He declared that, after the Hell Cycle ended on 16th August 1987 there would be a period of peace.

A planetary alignment known as the Harmonic Convergence occurred on 17th August 1987, 25 years before 2012. Thousands of lightworkers went to hilltops or sacred places on that day to pray or meditate for love and peace on Earth.

For me the Harmonic Convergence of 1987 was a magical time. The sunrise was the most awesome I have ever experienced, not so much for its brilliant orange beauty but for its majesty and energy. There were three of us who meditated together on a hilltop and we knew something had changed on the planet.

As a result of all the prayers and celebrations on that day, St Germain went to Source to intercede for humanity. He accessed the Violet Flame of Transmutation for the use of everyone, not just for the few who could use it up to that time. That is when the purification of the planet started.

Thousands of people used the energy of the Violet Flame and not only was their inner darkness transmuted but they were sending the energy to others and to the planet itself.

At the same time a wave of new transformational books was being published, enabling people to understand and change themselves. These were also empowering people to dissolve and heal their old attachments.

A few years later books on angels became more widely read, opening many to higher spiritual help and awareness. The angels asked me to tell people in my writing that they cannot help the planet or any of us unless we ask them to because they cannot contravene our free will. However, if you ask angels to help you they will as long as it is for your highest good. And if you request them to help someone else, your energy makes a link to that person along which they can work. It is then up to the person in need if they accept it.

If you ask angels to purify a specific place, they will pour their light into that area. The more often you do this, the more angels surround you waiting to work with you.

As this twenty-five year period started more spiritual people called on the assistance of the archangels for the purification of the world. Their angels flocked to all parts of the planet in response to these prayers. Many invoked Archangel Zadkiel to transmute stuck energy, and he and his angels used this opportunity to change the old. Groups of like-minded spiritual individuals started to gather to send out the light.

Our attention is being drawn in a variety of ways to land that needs to be purified. Here is an example of what happened in my garden:

Chafer beetles attacked the entire area in which I lived. Eventually I dug up a huge area and planted vegetables, which brought me a wonderful connection with the earth and the elementals, as well as a feeling of deep satisfaction. I allowed the grass to grow long to make it less attractive to the beetles and walked on it in bare feet as often as possible I realized that the beetles were drawing attention to the fact that the ground needed to be purified, so I invoked Archangel Gabriel to help. After that, every time I took photos of the garden there were Orbs of his angels of purification pouring light into the ground.

We are already seeing the start of the climatic changes as Lady Gaia is giving us warnings and wake-up calls. Each natural disaster reminds us to purify ourselves and the land on which we walk.

Here is a very simple exercise you can do daily, which will enable you to leave golden footsteps on the Earth wherever you go.

EXERCISE: *Golden Footsteps*

1. Invoke Archangel Gabriel and sense a pure white light pouring through you and into the Earth.
2. Invoke the Christ Light and sense a golden white light shimmering through you and into the Earth.
3. Ask that this energy stays with you all day and goes deeply into the soil wherever you walk.
4. As you go about your daily tasks, whether you are in a skyscraper or on the ground, your light can reach down into the ground and help to purify the world.

CHAPTER 3

The Year 2012

WHAT WILL HAPPEN IN 2012? We are told that, assuming we are ready, there will be a gradual but accelerated awakening as people raise their frequency. This does depend on people everywhere, which is why it is so important for lightworkers to focus on the good and hold a vision of the return of Golden Atlantis. Many of the prophecies have been challenging and we must rise above these and focus on the wonderful possibilities.

> *I think of 2012 as the quickening. It is the moment you feel the baby kicking in your womb and you know the transformation is for real. But you still have time for preparation before the new life emerges.*

The outcome depends on how many people prepare themselves by raising their vibrations for this momentous period and how they accept the energy of the cosmic moments. Based on the consciousness in 2009, the following is the probable outcome that we will experience.

~ Those in the Third Dimension ~

The vast masses in the third dimension, who are materialistic and spiritually closed, are holding everything back. Those souls who are not prepared will choose at the end of their current incarnation to continue their journey on another third-dimensional planet. They will depart with gratitude for the opportunity of being here.

However, right now huge numbers are being much influenced by the climate of change taking place worldwide. So, depending on the level of overall consciousness, many who currently believe only in a physical world, will awaken and open up psychically. Some will start to see or hear spirits, fairies or even angels and the Illumined Masters. Because their chakras will not be accustomed to the higher energy, it may confuse and terrify them. This will be especially so if their belief system or religious background has told them that there is no such dimension. Because of this the incidence of what we call mental illness could well increase. Many such people may become ungrounded and will need assistance.

We have already seen instances of those who cannot cope with the faster vibrations of light coming in. They are acting out their lower fantasies, which are exaggerated by the Internet. If you want to help these people you can assist greatly by blessing the worldwide web and sending light to it.

~ The Highest Possibilities for 2012 ~

The highest possibility is that a great many of those in the third dimension will open their heart chakras and be shifted by the light into the fourth dimension. When your heart is open you cannot hurt another, so this would result in peace movements spontaneously arising all over the planet. For these people, awakening to the spiritual worlds will be a wonderful expansion of their consciousness. With their hearts open they will automatically love and respect other cultures and animals, so that better conditions for children, animals and refugees will naturally occur worldwide. They will also move into an understanding of past lives, so beginning to remember who they truly are and appreciate their expanded soul journey. As they recognize their magnificence and worth they will begin to honour themselves and each other – and people with self-worth treat themselves and all beings with respect. There will be a feeling of Oneness with animals, plants and fellow humans. People will begin to feel their brotherhood/sisterhood and start to work for the common good.

A huge number will move onto their path to enlightenment and ascension.

~ Those in the Fourth Dimension ~

The greatest hope is that many of those currently in the fourth dimension will move into the fifth, where they will start to work for world peace, fairness and all sorts of humanitarian projects. Knowing it is time to alleviate world poverty, they will affect a huge change on the planet. We need to have a volume of people in the fifth dimension by 2012.

~ Those in the Fifth Dimension ~

The vast majority of those who are in the fifth dimension before 2012 will ascend, in other words carry the light of their I AM Presence, in their auras. They will remain at this higher frequency in their physical bodies, so that they can hold the light for everyone.

Some will decide to pass over and assist from the other side. But will they disappear in a flash of light? I do not think so.

~ Current Forecast for 2012 ~

My guide Kumeka says that the energies of dark and light are balanced and we must all focus on the positive to energize it and tip the balance to the side of light. We must take advantage of all the special alignments and energies being sent to us at this time to ensure we raise our frequency. Then there are awesome possibilities of wonderful things happening, including mass ascension, miraculous healings and great happiness for all.

~ The Influence of Obama on Ascension ~

In October 2008 Kumeka, my guide, said that, based on the consciousness then, 11% of the population would become enlightened and could ascend at the cosmic moment in 2012, most of them choosing to remain in a physical body carrying a higher level of light. After the wave of excitement at the U.S. elections in November 2008 the number increased to 14%. At Obama's inauguration the hope and anticipation was so strong that the forecast became 18%. It is anticipated that the number of people ascending will accelerate after 2012.

We can increase the 18% to a higher figure if we can help more people to open their twelve chakras and bring the light of Source through us into the Earth. We can also increase it if we bring hope and inspiration to our communities or to the world.

~ *The Higher Purpose of the Moon in 2012* ~

At the cosmic moments the Earth will be flooded by high frequency divine feminine energy from the moon. Those who can open up their right brain at this time and accept this energy will bring back the energy of Golden Atlantis. Because the moon vibrates at the frequency of the number 9, that of endings, it will tip the planet into ascension. Those who are psychic but not spiritually evolved may have a problem because they will open up more but not know what to do with the energy.

The full moon is on 28th November and 28th December 2012, round the cosmic moment on 21st December. This will result in exceptionally high tides, almost certainly triggering flooding in low-lying areas.

EXERCISE: *Moonlight Energy*

During the times of the full moon, even if you cannot see it because of clouds, walk outside in its light. Allow yourself to get accustomed to its energy, so that you can accept more of the divine feminine and are prepared for 2012.

CHAPTER 4

Why it will be Different this Time

MANY OF THE ANCIENT PREDICTIONS focused on catastrophe and disaster. This is because, at similar times in the history of the planet, the consciousness of humanity was so low that war or dire consequences resulted.

This time Lady Gaia, the great angel in charge of Earth, has decreed that the planet and all on her must rise in frequency and ascend. This is why the Spiritual Hierarchy has sent us much help in these end times to wake people up and enable many to move successfully into the new and faster frequencies:

1. On 8th June 2004 there was the first part of a double Venus transit. The second will be on the 6th June 2012. This wonderful and special conjunction starts to balance the masculine and feminine energy within individuals and in the collective consciousness. It includes the possibility of accelerating individual and planetary ascension and offers everyone huge opportunities for growth. However, this is a gift from God and it is important during the period between the two dates that we all help unite the world so that we can transform ourselves and the planet through spiritual awareness.

    This involves having respect for all forms of life and the planet's resources.

2. In November 2003 the Harmonic Concordance occurred which bestowed more divine feminine energy on everyone to awaken compassion and open hearts.

3. For the first time since the fall of Atlantis the twelve rays have been returned to Earth bathing us in higher light.

4. In 2008 the Silver Ray was sent to us by Source himself. This contains the highest aspect of the divine feminine and it merges with the other rays to balance them.

5. The Violet Flame of Transmutation was made available to everyone at the Harmonic Convergence in 1987. Since then the Gold and Silver Rays have synthesized with the Violet Flame to create the Gold and Silver Violet Flame, which holds people in the fifth dimension as it transmutes and raises the frequency.

6. The Gem Rays, containing pure Archangel energy can be invoked to fill us with light.

7. Many beings in Atlantis, including aspects of the twelve rays, the Christ energy, Buddha energy and the Spirit of Peace and Equilibrium contributed to a pool of light that the people could all access. Known as the Mahatma energy, it was abused at the end of Atlantis and withdrawn. This has now been returned to us. This is the highest energy that we can currently access and it accelerates our ascension dramatically. It is a very powerful golden white light, which heals on every level and can help with relationships and situations. It can never harm us as it is downloaded through our Monad or I AM Presence.

8. The Angels of Atlantis are helping us to bring back the wisdom of Golden Atlantis.

9. Fast frequency Universal Angels are coming to Earth. As our frequency speeds we can connect with them at a higher level, access more of their light and receive cosmic information.

10. Angels are impressing themselves as Orbs onto film, especially digital cameras, to offer us visible proof of their presence and to download messages and inspiration directly to us.

11. More enlightened children from Orion and wise old souls from many parts of the universes are being born.

12. The unicorns, the purest of the pure, have returned to seek those who have a vision to help others. Then they connect with them and assist their soul longings to come to fruition.

13. The unicorns are helping people to dissolve the veils of illusion that are blocking their third eyes, so they can reach full enlightenment. For full details see chapter 37.

EXERCISE: *Making a Difference*

Simply affirm to yourself that you can make a difference. Think about your life and how you live it, and find simple things that you can change for the better. Then act in such a way that you do. For example, you can smile at shop assistants, bless your water, spend five minutes each day appreciating the wonderful world we live in. Your aura will transform and your higher energy will touch others.

EXERCISE: *Visualization, Working with the Gem Rays*

The ruby is the materialized form of the ruby ray, containing the energy of Archangels Uriel and Aurora. It offers deep wisdom and knowledge, serenity and the energy to take action.

The emerald is the physical form of Archangels Raphael and Mary's ray. It offers balance, trust, healing, wisdom and higher spirituality.

The sapphire holds the light of Archangels Michael and Faith and the ray gives strength, ancient information and higher powers of communication.

The diamond is the materialization of the diamond ray of Archangels Gabriel and Hope. This is the ray of purity, clarity and divine purpose which takes people to higher dimensions.

1. Sit quietly where you will be undisturbed.
2. Decide which ray you wish to invoke.
3. Say or think, 'I now invoke the ruby/emerald/sapphire/diamond ray.'
4. Breathe the colour of your chosen gem ray into every cell of your body.
5. Ask the appropriate angels to add their blessings.
6. Sit for a few minutes allowing the blessings of this ray to touch you deeply
7. Thank the archangels.
8. Open your eyes.

CHAPTER 5

The Cosmic Moments

AS A WORLD we are about to experience two cosmic moments, during each of which there will be silence throughout the universe. At these times the portals of heaven will open to pour unimaginable high frequency light onto us, so that the possibilities are awesome and limitless. Both will occur in the morning at eleven minutes past eleven.

11.11 is a master number that indicates the beginning of a new phase at a much higher level. 11.11 was set up as an energy in the collective consciousness aeons ago, even before Atlantis and Lemuria, and it always starts the new in motion.

The first cosmic moment is at 11.11am on the 11th November 2011. This should be a time of celebration.

We are asked to celebrate our success to date and envision how wonderful it will be in 2012.

The second cosmic moment is at 11.11 am on 21st December 2012.

11.11 am on 21st December 2012 is a moment when great light will pour into the planet, and miracles and a further boost to enlightenment and ascension will occur. The shift will be energetic, so if you are expecting a cataclysm you may be relieved when it does not occur, while if you are anticipating instant illumination you will probably be disappointed. The opportunities arising as a result of this moment will be immense and sensitive people will feel it.

~ What to Do at the Cosmic Moments ~

Lord Melchizedck, who overlights the Diana Cooper School, has communicated that the whole world needs to start now to build up the energy for the cosmic moments. He said that the most effective way to prepare people would be to offer a prayer followed by an 11 minute 'ohm', followed by a one-minute silence during the moment. He gave us the Vision Prayer that you can find on page 30.

~ Law of Prayer ~

God is listening to you all the time, aware of everything you ask for with your thoughts, words or prayers. In this sense negative thoughts and worries are third-dimensional prayers. Whining, groveling, bargaining or manipulative requests to God or His angels are divinely disregarded.

However, affirmations, which are clearly verbalized, are very positive prayers. Be very careful what you ask for! Requests directed to God or through the angels are a hotline to the divine.

You listen to the universe in your meditations.

~ To Pray Effectively ~

1. Pray from your heart.

2. Ensure your intentions are pure.

3. Never tell God or the angels what you do not want or what you are suffering!!! If you do that you are asking for more of that which you do not want.

4. Tell God of your vision: "This is what I want to achieve. This is what I have already done. This is what I need from you."

5. Ask for the highest good to be done. If it really is for the highest good of all, the entire universe will rearrange itself to grant it. So detach from it being as you expect it to be or even from it happening at all. God may have something better in mind for you.

   Your prayer becomes even stronger when you ask others to pray with you and hold your vision.

~ *Gratitude Prayers* ~

These are fifth-dimensional prayers in which you give thanks with the faith that what you ask for is already granted. Then you enthusiastically prepare to receive it, as you know deep inside that it already is with you. Faith and gratitude are mighty energies that activate a response from heaven. In the fifth dimension you are living in a clear stream of divine consciousness, so you only ever ask for something that is for the highest good.

A collective prayer like the Vision Prayer for 2012 and beyond creates great light when said by many people and sends a constant stream of pure intention to the Godhead. If you possibly can, light a candle before you say it.

~ *The Vision Prayer* ~

I have a vision where all people are at peace, fed and
housed, every child is loved and educated to develop their
talents, where the heart is more important than the head
and wisdom is revered over riches.

In this world justice, equality and fairness rule.
Nature is honoured, so the waters flow pure and clear and
the air is fresh and clean. Plants and trees are nurtured
and all animals are respected and treated with kindness.
Happiness and laughter prevail

And humans walk hand in hand with angels.
Thank you for the love, understanding, wisdom, courage
and humility to do my part to spread the light.
May all the world ascend.
So be it.

EXERCISE: *Write a Personal Prayer*

You may like to write a prayer for your own personal vision. Keep it simple and sincere, and put your heart in it when you write it down. Then say your prayer three times alone or in your group. End by saying thank you and affirm: this is done.

CHAPTER 6

The Olympic Games in 2012

IN 2012 THE OLYMPIC GAMES will be held in London because this city is the spiritual Earth Star Chakra of the planet. The importance of this cannot be underestimated.

The Intergalactic Council has always known it had to take place there for the new light must be grounded deep in the Earth. The world would save much energy and hassle if governments and committees could allow choices like the location of the Olympic Games to arise automatically from attuned wisdom!

~ The Earth Star Chakra of the Planet ~

The Earth Star Chakras of all people and the planet are looked after by Archangel Sandalphon who is currently holding the kundalini energy for the world. Sandalphon and London vibrate on a number 1 energy, which energizes new beginnings. They are held in the influence of Sirius, also number 1. You will find more on the importance of numbers in chapter 40.

Within the Earth Star Archangel Sandalphon also nurtures the seeds of our potential. It is when we fully engage with the Earth by grounding ourselves and respecting the grass, trees, flowers, rocks and crystals that this chakra awakens and brings forward our divine possibilities.

Please see the chart on page 176 containing all the numbers, chakras, planetary locations, galactic connections and archangels. In addition, the chart on page 179 contains all the chakras, archangels, notes to attune to chakras and their fifth dimensional colours.

When all the other chakras are prepared and ready, the Earth Star triggers the Stellar Gateway, which is the ascension chakra, to open at the same time. This truth applies whether it is for individuals or the planet. In 2012 Earth will move to a higher level and accelerate its ascension.

The intention is that together as a world we raise our frequency during the Olympic Games. Then the spiritual kundalini of the planet, contained within the Earth Star will be triggered by the upsurge of excitement and hope until it is ready to rise at the cosmic moment.

It is anticipated that on 21st December 2012 the Earth Star Chakra and the Stellar Gateway of Earth will awaken, as forecast. Then the Stellar Gateway will fully expand like a chalice to receive an inpouring of Source energy! The entire planet can access and be bathed in Source light. What an opportunity for worldwide spiritual growth and transformation!

The original intention of the Olympic Games when it was set up in Golden Atlantis was to focus on celebration, togetherness and excellence. And those held in 2012 will bring much light to the world as a whole, not just London.

Please keep blessing the Olympic Games of 2012 and pray that enough energy is gathered during that time to enable the kundalini to rise as anticipated.

If you embrace this event as a bringer of light and hold it in the Golden Flame, you will add your energy to the highest possibilities. Even if you light only one candle to the success of the Olympic Games, you can make a difference. If you are reading this after that event, you can still light a candle to it, for Metatron will take your intention out of linear time in a divine perfect way to add to the whole.

Twenty years later, by 2032 the spiritual energy of the planet will be so high that choices for the highest good, such as the placement of important events, will arise automatically because the people will be aligned as one.

~ The Spiritual Stellar Gateway Chakra of Earth ~

The Stellar Gateway is in the Arctic, waiting to waken in 2012. This is where the Innuits live and for thousands of years have been containing the wisdom they brought from Golden Atlantis.

The High Priest, Sett, brought his tribe from Atlantis to this part of the world. They had a shamanic heritage and were very connected with the element of water. They chose to move to the Arctic because it would be covered by ice for approximately 4,000 years before 2012, so that the area would already be purified for them when the time was right.

During the Golden Age of Atlantis the Innuits had a symbiotic relationship with animals and many have maintained this. They can communicate with them and draw out their sacred knowledge to share with us all when enough people are ready. Because animals are going through their ascension process, just as we are, we will soon be able to help each other much more. Humans will no longer believe they are superior to any creature.

By 2032 the hearts of almost everyone will be open and exploitation of animals will be a thing of the past. Future generations will be appalled by what we have done to them but the animals will forgive us and we will share the planet in harmony again.

The elementals are in tune with London and the Arctic and are helping to prepare both areas for the massive new energy coming in during 2012 and beyond.

~ Location of the Spiritual Planetary Chakras ~

The planet has physical, mental, emotional and spiritual chakras, which is why there is so much discrepancy when people discuss them.

These are the twelve spiritual centres, each of which is connected to an Archangel. These places do not correspond to the locations of the Archangel retreats.

1.	EARTH STAR	London, UK
2.	BASE	Gobi Desert, China
3.	SACRAL	Honolulu
4.	NAVEL	Fiji
5.	SOLAR PLEXUS	Whole of South Africa
6.	HEART	Glastonbury, UK
	COSMIC HEART	Guatemala
7.	THROAT	Luxor, Egypt
8.	THIRD EYE	Afghanistan
9.	CROWN	Machu Picchu, Peru
10.	CAUSAL	Tibet
11.	SOUL STAR	Agra, India
12.	STELLAR GATEWAY	Arctic

The 12 Spiritual Chakras of the Planet

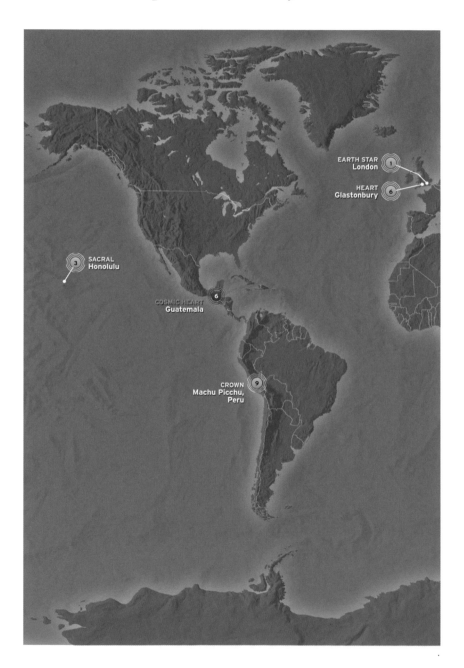

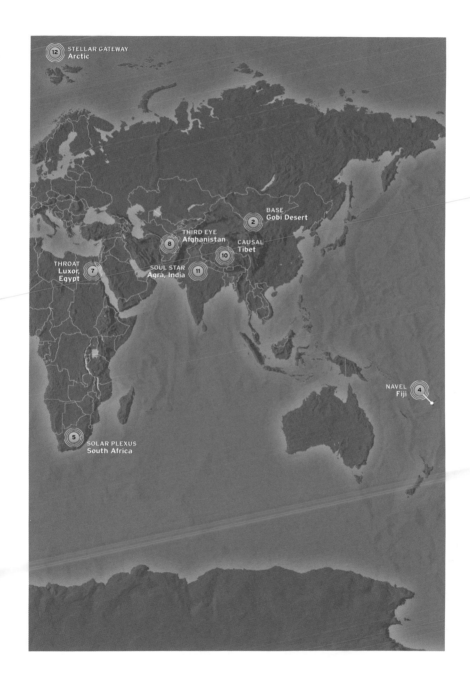

EXERCISE: *Visualization to Bless the Olympic Games*

1. Find a place where you can be quiet and undisturbed.
2. Close your eyes and relax.
3. Picture the Olympic flame in your mind's eye.
4. Send qualities of celebration, love, harmony, togetherness, excellence and joy to it.
5. See the flame expanding until its light spreads out into the cosmos.
6. Bless all the Olympic Games there ever have been and ever will be.
7. Open your eyes.

EXERCISE: *Discuss the Olympic Games*

With adults or children draw the flame of the Olympic Games and talk about the original purpose of the international event – to bring people together for celebration and to focus on harmony, joy and excellence. Your energy will add to that of the Games and enable the planetary kundalini to rise.

CHAPTER 7

Cosmic Portals opening in 2012

LOCATED ALL OVER THE WORLD are massive cosmic portals, most of which will be bursting open in 2012. Some are slumbering ready to wake up gently, possibly before then. Others will wake a little later. But they will all have a huge impact on the surrounding areas and on the whole world as their high frequency light spreads.

There are thirty-three of these cosmic portals, so they bring in the Christ light as well as the twelve rays and the Silver Ray of the Divine Feminine.

Imagine a tree with the trunk coming down through the centre of the Earth. Above, the branches reach out linking to the planets and stars. Below, the roots spread out through the Earth to specific points. These are cosmic leylines.

The light of the twelve rays, merged with the Silver Ray, flows down from the cosmos, through the branches and trunk and then spreads through each of these roots to the portals, which are ready to open. There it rises like a fountain to saturate the land and its people in divine light. Visualizing this will help to energize the process of preparing the planet for the cosmic moment in 2012.

There are also many smaller portals opening at this time, where there have been standing stones, sacred sites or places of great natural beauty. These will not usually bring in the Christ Light like the 33 cosmic portals.

The 33 Cosmic Portals

~ Ancient Cultures ~

1. ATLANTIS – this portal is already opening, waking up the energy of the Temple of Poseidon in the Atlantic Ocean and bringing forward the wisdom of Atlantis.

2. LEMURIA – this portal is already opening in Hawaii activating the great crystal of Lemuria and returning the wisdom it holds.

3. HOLLOW EARTH – this portal in the centre of the Earth is just beginning to open and will profoundly affect the leylines. It is an elongated oval in the U.S. covering Oklahoma, Kansas, Nebraska, South Dakota and southern North Dakota. Originally it was a huge round circle but the shape changed as it was squashed by everything moving within and under the earth. The energy entering in 2012 is high enough and strong enough to support its return to its original shape and size and this will impact on the people. It will be a long slow opening. By 2032 it will be 93% ready; it will reach its full glory by 2035 when there will be enormous activity both physically and energetically in this area.

   There are other entries to the Hollow Earth but this one in America is the main portal that lined up with the centre of the universe, which is the seat of Source, at the time when it was originally opened. It will align once more into its original position in 2035, will stay fully open for three years, and then recede slowly. So it builds up, opens and then slowly closes like a flower but its impact will be enormous. This portal in America will close because the Earth's movement means that it is no longer aligned to the centre of the universe. Then another of the entry points to Hollow Earth in a different part of the planet will open.

4. MU – this portal in the Pacific Ocean is closed, opening in 2012, re-awakening the latent wisdom of the ancient civilization of Mu.

~ Australasia ~

5. **ULURU, AUSTRALIA** – connecting with Aborigine wisdom. Opening in 2012.

6. **FIJI** – connecting with Maori wisdom. This is where the Atlanteans went at the fall of their continent, before they continued to New Zealand. Opening in 2012.

~ Americas ~

7. **SEDONA, USA** – connecting with Native American wisdom. Opening in 2012.

8. **THE BERMUDA TRIANGLE** – the Great Crystal of Atlantis was a portal, amongst other things, held within the Temple of Poseidon. When Atlantis fell, the crystal lodged at the bottom of the ocean in the middle of the Bermuda Triangle. If the Intergalactic Council needs to use it, it is opened and everyone and everything within it go through a rapid interdimensional shift. To human eyes they tragically disappear but at a soul level anyone involved agrees to this experience. So this portal is sometimes open and at other times closed.

9. **BANFF, CANADA** – opening in 2012.

10. **ALASKA, ARCTIC** – connecting with Innuit wisdom. Opening in 2012.

11. **THE SOUTH POLE** – opening in 2012.

~ South America ~

12. **MAYAN SETTLEMENT IN HONDURAS** – already opening.

13. **THE WHOLE OF PERU** – connecting with Inca wisdom. Opening in 2012.

~ Africa ~

14. **MALI** – connecting with the Dogon wisdom. After Ra brought his tribe from Atlantis to Egypt, the Dogons, who were a part of that group, moved further down Africa and settled in Malawi. They carried with them wisdom and ancient knowledge from Sirius and still hold it for us all now. The portal is sleeping, opening in 2012.

15. **THE SPHINX AT EGYPT** – opening in 2012.

~ The Middle East ~

16. **MESOPOTAMIA** – opening after 2012, bringing back the wisdom of Golden Atlantis that was brought here by the tribe of Apollo after the fall.

~ The Far East ~

17. **THE SOURCE OF THE GANGES, INDIA** – slumbering ready to open before 2012.

18. **VARANASI, INDIA** – beginning to open now.

19. **MANILA, PHILIPPINES** – opening in 2012.

20. **MONGOLIA** – opening in 2012.

21. **ANGKOR WAT, CAMBODIA** – this portal is slumbering preparing to wake before 2012.

22. Quan Yin where she held the energy in the mountains along **THE SILK ROAD** – asleep, opening in 2012.

23. **WUHAM IN EASTERN CHINA** – opening in the period from 2012 to 2014.

24. **ANSI IN NORTHERN CHINA** – opening in 2012.

~ *Europe* ~

25. **YORK**, in the Yorkshire dales, UK – this is a huge portal, opening in 2012.

26. **ANDORRA** – this portal is sleeping, opening in 2012.

27. Under the water **OFF THE COAST OF MARSEILLES** – opening soon after 2012.

~ *Russia* ~

28. **OMSK IN THE URALS** – opening in 2012.

29. **SIBERIA** – opening in 2012.

30. **AGATA, NORTHERN RUSSIA** – opening in 2012.

31. **OPALA ON KAMCHATKA ISLAND, RUSSIA** – opening in 2014.

32. **GORA CHEN IN THE KERKEYANSK RANGE, RUSSIA** – already beginning to open.

33. **NORTH POLE, ANTARCTIC** – this one is beginning to open now.

All these portals apart from the one in Hollow Earth will rest after a few years because they have accimilated and shared with our planet as much cosmic energy as they can cope with. When they have rested they will re-open.

The 33 Cosmic Portals

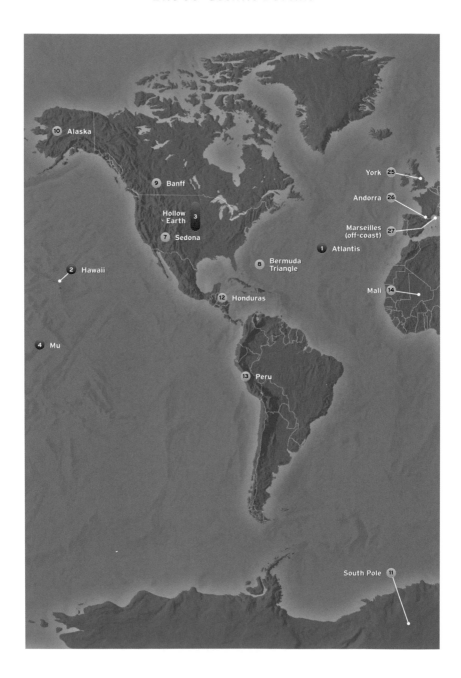

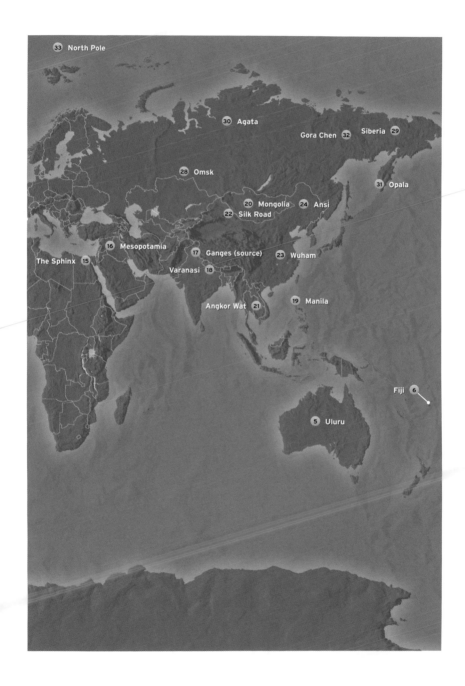

~ *The Twelve Rays* ~

These high frequency rays of light are strands of God force, which are now being poured into the Earth for the benefit of everyone. In addition, in 2008 the Silver Ray, the Divine Feminine Ray, merged with all the other rays to balance them. The archangels often work on a different aspect of the rays from the Masters, which is why some rays have more than one colour.

RAY 1 is red and the Master is El Morya, influencing people to use their divine will rather than their lower will and to empower themselves. Archangel Michael works on the blue aspect of ray 1.

RAY 2 is yellow (sometimes blue) and is in the charge of Lanto. It is the ray of love and wisdom, for its frequency helps people to communicate Truth wisely. Archangel Jophiel, angel of wisdom, works on the yellow ray.

RAY 3 is golden yellow and the Master is Paul the Venetian. The vibration of this ray of intelligence and creative activity brings forward creativity and helps to trigger science and wisdom. Archangel Chamuel, angel of love, works on the pink aspect of this ray.

RAY 4 brings about harmony and balance on an amethyst and white vibration under the direction of Serapis Bey. Archangel Gabriel, angel of purity and clarity, works on the pure white of this ray.

RAY 5 is orange and the Master is Hilarion. The ray is helping to bring forward spiritual technology and science, all the secrets of which are hidden in nature. Archangel Raphael, angel of healing and abundance, works on the emerald green aspect of this ray.

RAY 6 is indigo under the direction of Mary Magdalene and is opening the world up to true spirituality. Archangel Uriel, angel of peace, works on the gold and purple aspect of this ray.

RAY 7 is violet under the guidance of Lady Nada. Its frequency is bringing forward the ancient healing techniques, awakening sacred wisdom and intuition and higher psychic energies. Archangel Zadkiel also works on the violet aspect of this ray to bring transmutation.

RAY 8 is blue topaz. It is in the charge of Kumeka, Lord of Light, who is my guide. This ray brings about enlightenment and transmutation of the old. Archangel Butyalil works on the white aspect of this ray.

RAY 9. This is the yellow ray of harmony, which entered the planet in 2001 and balances the mind and spirit of humanity. Vosloo, the greatest High Priest in Atlantis, is the Master of this ray. Seraphina, of the seraphim frequency, is the angelic being who works on this ray and she vibrates on every colour.

RAY 10. This is the citrine ray, which entered the planet at the end of 2001, and helps people to find their practical purpose in life. It carries the Buddha energies and Lord Gautama is in charge of this ray. Archangel Sandalphon works with the unicorns on this ray with black and white energy.

RAY 11. This bright emerald green ray brings clarity, mysticism and healing. It is bringing spirituality to dogmatic religions and helping us to accept the higher energies coming in. This ray entered the planet at the end of 2001 and Rakoczy is its Master. Archangel Christiel works on this ray on the colour ice white, tinged with blue.

RAY 12. Quan Yin is the master of this ray of unconditional love, which entered the planet in 2003. The colour is bright cerise pink. It carries a frequency to re-empower women and bring forward the feminine wisdom within men. Archangel Metatron works with his orange light on this ray.

EXERCISE: *The Cosmic Tree and Portals*

1. Sit and relax where you can be undisturbed.
2. Hold the intention of energizing the Cosmic Tree and awakening the portals.

3. Visualize the trunk of a tree coming down right through the planet.
4. Branches from the tree trunk reach out to touch the bright stars, which fill the vast sky above.
5. Light from the 12 rays merged with the Silver Ray pours down through the branches and trunk. Red, yellow, deep yellow, amethyst–white, orange, indigo, violet, topaz blue, yellow, citrine, emerald, cerise pink and silver.
6. The light spreads out along all the roots throughout the world.
7. Where it reaches one of the portals, a huge fountain of light shimmering with all these colours rises through the surface of the Earth and cascades over the area.
8. Sense the light waking up everything and everyone it touches.
9. As everyone wakes, see the whole world holding hands.
10. Give thanks for this and open your eyes.

You can also visualize yourself as the Cosmic Tree. I love doing this visualization. it seems so important and special. I also love the energy, which flows through me.

EXERCISE: *Visualize Yourself as a Cosmic Tree*

1. Sit and relax where you can be undisturbed.
2. Hold the intention of energizing the Cosmic Tree and awakening the portals.
3. Visualize your body as the trunk of the Cosmic Tree.
4. See the branches reaching out from your crown to the stars.
5. Light from the twelve rays merged with the Silver Ray pours down through the branches and then through your body. Red, yellow, deep yellow, amethyst–white, orange, indigo, violet, topaz blue, yellow, citrine, emerald, cerise pink and silver.
6. The light spreads out along your roots and throughout the world.
7. Where it reaches one of the portals, a huge fountain of light shimmering with all these colours rises through the surface of the Earth and cascades over the area.
8. Sense the light waking up everything and everyone it touches.
9. As everyone wakes, see the whole world celebrating.
10. Give thanks for this and open your eyes.

CHAPTER 8

The Crystal Skulls in 2012

IN GOLDEN ATLANTIS twelve crystal skulls, one for each of the tribes, were fashioned using the sort of spiritual technology that will eventually return to us. Each came from a solid piece of quartz and was created by the use of mind control and thought power; a technique that at the moment is not accessible to our currently untrained and only fractionally used minds.

The skulls were the size of our human one and had a jaw that moved. Within the crystal was an extraordinary network of prisms and lenses, which lit up the face and eyes.

They were able to speak and sing because they were advanced computers programmed with all the knowledge and wisdom of their tribe. The High Priests and Priestesses also entered into them esoteric information about human origins and the mysteries of life. This was so that the true history of the planet would not be lost. Most importantly the skulls hold the vision of unity consciousness, and those who are touched by their energy will feel this even from a distance.

When people have a sufficiently high frequency, they will be able to tune into the skulls and read the files they contain.

The knowledge held within the skulls was considered so important that it was all placed within one amethyst Master skull, of a very high vibration. When Atlantis fell, the amethyst skull was dematerialized and taken into the inner planes. It will only return when the planet is ready for it, as if we were to access it now in our current state of consciousness we would do immeasurable damage.

All the files of information for this planet from the beginning of time are held in a high frequency band within the Sphinx. The information that is held in the skulls was also placed within the Sphinx. Again this will be read on a psychic level when people are ready to tune into it.

As Atlantis was being destroyed the priestesses took the crystal skulls for their tribes with them to the new destinations prepared for the survivors. Here they were hidden to be revealed when the time is right. So far only one has surfaced.

~ The Mayan Skull ~

One skull has been released, the Mayan one, known as the skull of love, programmed with all the wisdom of the tribe that was led by Aphrodite. She originated from Venus, planet of love, and her people understood the movements of Venus. When she took her survivors to South America, they became the Mayans who brought with them from Atlantis their knowledge of astronomy and mathematics. This is why they had the special information which allowed them to calculate the Mayan calendar, covering the period from 3114 BC to 2012 AD, with its incredibly accurate prophecies. Their knowledge enabled them to build their nine step pyramids perfectly aligned to the stars. Each of the nine steps depicts a transformational leap for humankind since the beginning of time and every section tells us exactly where our planetary consciousness is – right up to 2012.

These pyramids are cosmic computers, which are designed to be activated in 2012 by the energy of the stars. They will then wake up latent powers within the skulls.

Each of the Mayan Temples and their adjoining settlements was totally self-sufficient. The information they brought with them from Atlantis was not only esoteric but also practical, so they knew exactly how to grow food not just in conventional ways but with methods currently out of our awareness.

The ancient Mayans held the wisdom of Golden Atlantis in their consciousness. However, that wisdom, which the astronomers and astrologers had then and partly have now, could also be used for dark purposes They could, for example, harm others by the use of right timing for attack. As the Mayans were invaded by many tribes whose consciousness was too low to use this knowledge wisely, they decided to leave the planet. They ascended taking the wisdom from Atlantis with them, apart from the sacred files hidden within the crystal skull.

The Mayans thought they left the area protected and highly charged. They intended it to be a place where people could come and go for a long time, immersing themselves in the high frequency energy and taking it out with them. They believed this would hold the continent in peace and subtly influence the world beyond. However, the consciousness of those remaining in the surrounding areas quickly dropped. Beings from Venus did step in to try to reverse the trend but the general darkness on the planet blocked their intervention.

After discussions on the inner planes, the Intergalactic Council decided to release the Mayan skull, hoping they could reverse the downward trend on Earth and dissolve the energy of war that was hanging like a cloud over the world.

So the awesome Mayan skull containing wondrous information that we can scarcely begin to access or understand was released in 1927. Anna Mitchell-Hedges was a young girl who was helping her father, an archaeologist, to explore one of the lost Mayan cities deep within the rainforests of the ancient ruin of Lubaantum, now in Belize. She discovered the skull under an altar and was its keeper until she died. It is now in the charge of Bill Homann.

~ The Incan Skull ~

Thoth, later known as Hermes Trismegistus was the High Priest who took the crystal skull from Atlantis to Peru. He taught that there is harmony and correspondence in every living thing in the universe, including the movement of planets, tides and currents, animals, plants, crystals and everything. The entire cosmos responds to certain harmonies and combinations of notes, which are tuned to the same scale. When the notes are correct there is perfect balance and healing. His immense and detailed knowledge is held within the Incan crystal skull and will in due course bring total alignment and healing to the natural world, animals and humans when we can access it and have the consciousness to understand and use it.

When the Atlanteans arrived in South America they became the Incas, who built the mighty two way interdimensional portal of Machu Picchu. As with the Mayans, the priests all ascended believing they had left the portal protected. I describe the esoteric secrets of Machu Picchu in the first of my trilogy of novels, The Silent Stones.

> *The Atlantis crystal skull taken to Peru will be found there before 2012 by a group, who will be its true custodians. They will recognize it and because they know the impact of its power they will maintain it securely and privately and keep it sacred.*

Although people in the wider environs will not know about it, it will affect the consciousness everywhere with the wisdom and light it radiates and help to raise the energy for 2012.

Some sensitive people will be able to pick up the light the skull is radiating and will be able to use some of the spiritual information and knowledge contained within it.

After 2032 much of the world will use the wisdom of Thoth to maintain perfect health and keep their plants and animals healthy too.

Other crystal skulls have been found. These are not Atlantean but were created by the Magi of the tribe that left Atlantis and went to Egypt under the High Priest Ra. These later skulls are programmed with information that is not as pure or as comprehensive as that of the original skulls.

By 2032 six of the original Atlantean crystal skulls will have surfaced and will have a subtle impact on the spiritual consciousness of the world. It is possible to meditate on these skulls and ask that you be allowed access to information with which you can help the world.

EXERCISE: *Meditation on the Crystal Skulls*

1. Find a place where you can be quiet and undisturbed.
2. Light a candle and dedicate it to your vision or to world service.
3. For a few minutes relax your body on the outbreath until you feel really comfortable.
4. Ask to connect to one of the crystal skulls and visualize a silver thread linking you to it.
5. Sense your third eye. You may see colours or feel a sensation or you may not be aware of it opening.
6. You may receive a flash of insight or a comfortable feeling of being connected to higher wisdom. Or information may come to you later.
7. When you come to the end of your meditation thank the crystal skull.
8. Return to full waking consciousness.

CHAPTER 9

The Twelve
Ascension Chakras

OPENING THE TWELVE CHAKRAS is essential for the journey to ascension and enlightenment. It is basic preparation for 2012 so that you will be ready for the high energy coming in at that time.

In Golden Atlantis we had twelve chakras, carrying much higher light and wisdom than we currently have. When they are open the twelve strands of DNA start to be activated. These contain awesome latent psychic and spiritual gifts, which are waiting to return to us as soon as we awaken, open and activate the twelve chakras. This is why it is so important to understand and work with them again.

~ The Earth Star ~

The Earth Star is looked after by Archangel Sandalphon. It is about twelve inches or 30 cms below your feet and is black and white (yin-yang) in colour. Here all your potential for your lifetime is held rather like seeds in the ground. Archangel Sandalphon nurtures them and it is your responsibility to help in this. Every time you walk on the earth in bare feet or go walking in the countryside, you help this chakra to develop. As it does so the seeds of your divine possibilities also grow.

In addition the Earth Star is the foundation for your spiritual growth. Because you cannot go higher than you can dig deep, it is important to establish this chakra. There are two Universal Angels who take the energy of this centre right into the middle of the Earth and anchor it there. These are Roquiel, who is black and of the divine feminine and Gersisa, who is grey and inhabits the Hollow Earth. They anchor the energy of the Earth Star to the centre of the Earth. Both these Universal Angels are very active now in helping us to establish this very strong spiritual foundation.

When all your other chakras are ready, including the twelfth one, the Stellar Gateway, your Earth Chakra ignites. Only then can your Stellar Gateway light up and open fully.

~ *The Base Chakra* ~

At the fifth-dimensional level this chakra is platinum and links you to the wisdom of the dolphins. When the kundalini rises and enters this chakra your life becomes grounded in joy and delight. You feel totally safe and trust the universe totally to look after you. Archangel Gabriel looks after this chakra and when all your lower fears are purified in this centre and the sacral and naval, you find new clarity and purpose.

~ *The Sacral Chakra* ~

Slightly above the base chakra and also in the charge of Archangel Gabriel this chakra is luminous pale pink. It is about transcendent sexuality and expressing tender, true love.

When this chakra opens at a fifth-dimensional level your relationships change as you are no longer sending out demands or neediness but are radiating higher, confident, loving energy.

~ *The Navel Chakra* ~

Glowing orange at the fifth dimension and also looked after by Archangel Gabriel, this chakra expresses a warm welcome for all people, sociability and acceptance.

~ *The Solar Plexus* ~

Radiating deep gold the solar plexus sends out peace, wisdom and the ability to soothe and calm people and situations. Archangel Uriel holds this centre in his light.

~ *The Heart Chakra* ~

The fifth-dimensional centre of the heart chakra is pure white in the care of Archangel Chamuel. Sending out only pure love, you see everyone and everything with eyes of love. You connect with the cosmic heart.

~ The Throat Chakra ~

When this chakra glows royal blue you automatically receive the protection, strength and courage of Archangel Michael. You now work with him and carry his blue cloak as well as his Sword of Truth and Shield of Protection, which you use to help others.

~ The Third Eye ~

The all-seeing eye is totally transparent at the fifth dimension, like a crystal ball, so you are preparing for your journey to enlightenment. Archangel Raphael offers you gifts of healing and abundance.

~ The Crown Chakra ~

You now wear the crystal crown of the thousand-petalled lotus on your head, which opens fully allowing you to bring down light from your soul and feed it to the lower chakras. Archangel Jophiel is in charge of this centre.

~ The Causal Chakra ~

This pure white chakra above and slightly behind the crown is where you enter the silence. Archangel Christiel looks after it, when it is open and receptive beings of the higher spiritual realms drop their guidance and seeds of wisdom into your consciousness.

~ The Soul Star Chakra ~

This chakra works in two ways: Archangel Zadkiel transmutes ancestral karma, which is held in the lower section. When it opens, Archangel Mariel then brings forward the wisdom of your soul, which you can access in your daily life. This chakra is the magenta colour of the divine feminine.

~ The Stellar Gateway ~

Archangel Metatron, called Prince of the Countenance because he is the only angel allowed to look directly into the light of God, is in charge of your ascension journey. He works with your Stellar Gateway chakra, which is a beautiful golden colour. When this opens you start to access light from Source.

Just as you have two Universal Angels helping to anchor the energy of the Earth Star deeper into the planet, you have two helping to connect the Stellar Gateway to Source. The first is Seraphina, who is of the seraphim frequency. She helps Metatron to fine-tune the energies in the Stellar Gateway. Then she starts to build the ladder from Source down to the Stellar Gateway. When it is complete, she helps you to climb it. She also has a chakra within another dimension, which is an intergalactic training school and you can train here to be a cosmic Ambassador for Earth if you desire. Working with Metatron and Seraphina is Butyalil who is helping to align the cosmic currents that hold Earth in place.

EXERCISE: *Awakening your Earth Star*

1. Stand with your feet firmly on the ground hip-width apart.
2. Focus on your feet and imagine energy going down from them like the sides of a downward pointing triangle until they meet twelve inches or 30 cm below the ground.
3. Then put your attention on the toes, then right side of the feet, then the heel, then the left side of the feet. Continue to do this slight swaying until you feel your Earth Star is anchored.
4. Then place your mind in your Earth Star. Visualize it like a chamber below your feet, shining and luminous.
5. Be aware of the seeds of your potential growing within the chamber.
6. Here your kundalini is held.
7. Below it is a link right down into the centre of the Earth.

~ Activating the Twelve Chakras with the Fifth-dimensional Colours and Angels ~

You can do this formally as below but when you get to know the chakras you can do it while out walking, sitting in a train, plane or as a passenger in a car. It is very simple and the more often you do it, the more you anchor, open and activate your ascension chakras.

1. Light a candle if possible.

2. Sit quietly where you can be undisturbed.

3. Focus on your Earth Star Chakra below your feet and ask Archangel Sandolphon to connect with you. Pause until you can sense he is with you. Then breathe in and out of your black and white Earth Star Chakra three times.

4. Focus on your base chakra at your pubic bone and ask Archangel Gabriel to connect with you. Pause until you can sense he is there. Then breathe in and out of your platinum base chakra three times.

5. Move your awareness to your sacral chakra and ask Archangel Gabriel to enter it. Then breathe in and out of your pale pink sacral chakra three times.

6. Move up to your navel chakra and invite Archangel Gabriel to move into it. Then breathe in and out of your luminous orange navel chakra three times.

7. Focus on your solar plexus and call in Archangel Uriel to hold the energy of wisdom here. Then breathe in and out of your deep golden solar plexus chakra three times.

8. Rise to your heart chakra and invite Archangel Chamuel to waken you to pure love. Then breathe in and out of your pure white heart chakra three times.

9. As you focus on your throat centre, call in Archangel Michael to touch you here. Then breathe in and out of your royal blue throat chakra three times.

10. Concentrate on your third eye and let Archangel Raphael assist you here. Then breathe in and out of your crystal-clear third eye three times.

11. Let your consciousness shift to your crown. Be aware of Archangel Jophiel, the angel of wisdom, opening your chakra wider. Then breathe in and out of your crystal-clear crown three times.

12. You are now activating your transcendent chakras above your head, so be aware of your pure white causal chakra and let Archangel Christiel help you. Then breathe in and out of it three times.

13. A little higher is your Soul Star chakra, which is magenta pink. Be aware of Archangel Mariel working with you, and breathe in and out of it three times.

14. It is time to move to your Stellar Gateway. Call in Archangel Metatron and sense him expanding your ultimate chakra. Then breathe in and out of this golden ball of light three times.

15. Thank the archangels for their help in activating your chakras and open your eyes.

CHAPTER 10

Lemuria and Mu

~ Mu ~

Many people talk of Mu as Lemuria and think the name is an abbreviation. However Mu was a civilization before Lemuria and was also centered in the Pacific Ocean. The people were of the fourth- to fifth-dimensional consciousness and were not physicalized so there are no remains. They tended the trees and plants and also worked with crystals but much less than the Lemurians.

The people of Mu were not as evolved as the civilization that followed them. They were happy to be here and experience Earth, to connect with the animals and touch on the physicality of this plane but they had no burning desire to heal the Earth like the Lemurians.

~ Lemuria ~

The Lemurian energy was strongest in Australia and New Zealand, Hawaii and the Polynesian Islands, part of Alaska and the north east of Africa. In Africa a little of Lemuria can be found in Morocco and part of Guinea. Mauritania, Algeria, Mali, and Senegal were fully Lemurian.

Because they drew light directly from the four ascension planets, Sirius, Orion, the Pleiades and Neptune, the energy of the Lemurians was very pure and innocent and healed the areas to which they were connected. Each of these stars, constellations and planets linked to a different part of the world and these places were 'populated' by Lemurians, who were not fully physicalized. Nevertheless they were affected by the people and the Earth in these places.

Lemurians were fifth-dimensional beings, though not fully in their physical bodies as we are. They were very tall and thin, blond with blue eyes.

Because they were more ethereal than physical their consciousness was focussed on the spiritual dimensions. They were androgynous, without sexuality and complete in themselves. Lemurians were harmonious peaceful beings, with open hearts that allowed them to express unconditional love to the divine and all of creation. Their great gift was Earth healing and they also programmed crystals with unconditional love and cosmic connections. Some of these crystals within the Earth are record keepers and they also form cosmic grids, linking planet Earth to the stars.

They were very connected to the physical earth and loved it, so bringing back your Lemurian wisdom involves touching the soil, walking and really enjoying the feel of the ground beneath you. They were also very attuned to the elemental kingdom.

~ Healing in Lemuria ~

We are told it is important now to activate anyone who has been in Lemuria, so that they can bring forward their healing gifts. At this moment this is needed to heal the faults in the Earth.

Lemurian healing was always done by more than one person at a time. Like all energies it can be used for good or ill, which is why those from ancient Lemuria are asked to connect with the unicorns for they will only work with people who will use the energy correctly. Although, according to Kumeka, this is not a complete safeguard for, like Reiki, this special healing power can be used now without understanding.

Individuals can programme a crystal and direct it to cleanse the crystals in the Earth, especially in Africa but it is not as powerful as it is when they do it in a group.

~ The Clearance of Neptune to Bring in Lemurian Healing ~

When Atlantis collapsed there was huge fear, which was taken to Neptune and held in the ice there. In addition, at the time of Christ, Neptune was cut away from the other four ascension planets, Orion, Sirius and the Pleiades. This blocked the wisdom of Atlantis from coming through and also the wisdom and healing power from Lemuria. As a result of prayer and meditation by many dedicated people, started by the teachers of the Diana Cooper School, who were particularly asked by spirit to do this as they are carefully trained, Neptune has been unblocked and fully connected again. The final connection was made during a glorious ceremony in Ireland, after which the teachers took blessed water from the celebration to the great portal at Tara, which is linked to Neptune. Now we can bring Lemurian healing through directly from Neptune. It is especially powerful in those portals and sacred places connected with that glorious blue healing planet of high spirituality.

Lemurian healing energy has ten times the power of Reiki.

If you want to do Lemurian healing you need to receive some training or practice to do the work co-operatively without a leader. It must be done in a group , which acts as one.

This energy was always used to heal the Earth but it can be used to heal people. However it may be too strong for them, so it needs to be offered with caution.

Lemurian healing is very important and needs to start happening before 2012 to help the planet.

If you wish to form a Lemurian healing group these are the steps:

– Check you were in Lemuria, either by listening to your intuition or by asking a psychic.

– Go to a good clairvoyant to check that your energy levels are right for this work.

– Ask the universe to bring other people on a similar level to you.

~ The Healing ~

1. Affirm that while the group is together you hold Lemurian light.

2. Connect to the unicorns and surrender to their energy.

3. Know that when you are working as a unit you are all switched on. When you separate you all automatically switch off.

4. The group will receive a collective message about the healing you are to send. No individual takes the lead. You all become one.

5. Together focus your healing energy on a particular place, according to the guidance you have received.

6. Thank the unicorns.

7. Open your eyes and return to the room.

The Transition Period
2012 – 2032

CHAPTER 11

World Economy

FOR A LONG TIME the financial system of the world has been like a rotten log. When those sitting on it fell off, they tried to scramble back onto the same crumbling log instead of seeking a new sound one.

In 2007 the banking and credit crisis started, with banks collapsing and businesses going bankrupt. The whole system based on greed, gambling, corruption and trampling on the poor could not continue. Exactly in accordance with the time line predicted in the Mayan calendar, the economic structure all started to collapse.

Within twenty years the concept of lending non-existent money and charging interest on it will be considered breathtakingly arrogant and corrupt. The principle of rich and poor will be unimaginable. There will be no banks or financial institutions.

The way that the banks, financial institutions and many businesses work is not aligned to the highest good and must adapt to accommodate the new paradigm.

The economies are collapsing because the frequency of the planet has moved up a gear spiritually and the cogs of old and new are no longer in synch. In order for them to synchronize, the world economy must move at a faster frequency, in other words with more honour, openness, honesty and fairness.

The system will continue to collapse and evolve until an economic structure based on fairness and integrity is in place. Then this too will dissolve as money ceases to have relevance after 2032.

~ Redundancies or Unemployment ~

Where an individual's work is not allowing him to express his highest truth, his soul will move him out of the old job or business. This is happening now en masse, coinciding with the rise in frequency of many and the collapsing economies. However, nothing happens by chance, and redundancy or unemployment is a wake-up call for all those affected, prompting them to seek a living, which aligns to their soul and brings them satisfaction. Those who raise their frequency and attune to the higher energies available will find their soul work, which will automatically come to them under the Law of Attraction.

By 2032 the majority who live in fifth-dimensional communities will occupy themselves in a way, which honours and respects their gifts and talents. For the first time since Golden Atlantis most people will enjoy soul satisfaction in their daily lives.

~ Trade after 2032 ~

During the twenty-year transition the challenges of travel in the new conditions will mean it is no longer be economically viable or sustainable to export food or goods around the world. Farmers will grow crops for local consumption, so that the vast acreage of mono- crops will be a thing of the past.

Some of those economies, which rely totally on exports, will need to be flexible and seek their inner strength.

Based on the current forecasts, by 2032 the world as we know it will have changed beyond recognition. There will no longer be international trade.

The new energies available will offer enormous opportunities for spiritual growth; so many more of those countries whose finances are currently based on exports will find their citizens are seeking spiritual enrichment instead. Because of this they will automatically attract to their higher frequencies all the abundance they need.

Because the majority in the world will be living in the fifth dimension, communities will be co-operating and sharing for the highest good, so there will be no need for money. Instead goods will be exchanged locally.

~ Big Businesses ~

These are the dinosaurs of our time. As the ethos of finance and business change, the huge businesses will continue to collapse. The companies that were household names will be memories by 2032. All companies that exploit people, animals or the land will disappear. Big supermarkets will be a thing of the past.

Only those companies that accommodate the changing frequency of the planet and operate for the highest good of all will survive, although in a very different form from that of their current modus operandi.

~ The New Business Paradigm ~

This is based on creating or producing for the highest good of the community and the planet. As most people will be living at a fifth-dimensional level, there will be an emphasis on co-operation, seeing the best in others and empowering them, offering excellence and each person contributing in a way that makes their heart sing.

Those businesses that honour everyone concerned and actively promote the good of animals, the nature kingdom and humanity will continue to be successful during the transition period.

~ International Co-operation ~

Soon rich people will no longer feel able to sit back and allow children or adults to work in sweatshops or for slave wages to provide them with material goods. Led by the people there will be a huge move by richer countries to help those that are less fortunate, and this will help to balance the enormous divides worldwide.

By 2022 there will be massive international co-operation on many fronts and terrible working conditions will no longer be tolerated.

EXERCISE: *Visualization for World Harmony*

1. Sit quietly where you can relax in peace.
2. Close your eyes and breathe deeply.
3. Ask the angels to help bring you into harmonic alignment with the work that will satisfy your soul.
4. Imagine yourself doing work that truly satisfies you. It may be

something totally different from your current job. Feel yourself happy, well rewarded and appreciated.

5. Spread this feeling to everyone you know and picture them happy in their work.
6. Now visualize everyone in the world in harmony with their daily lives. See them singing in their offices, in the fields or wherever they are.
7. Then open your eyes and smile.

CHAPTER 12

Power Supplies and Travel

~ Electricity ~

As people's frequencies rise in 2012 it will play havoc with electricity. Keep backing up your computer!

When an individual makes a leap in consciousness the changed frequency affects their electrical goods, which go haywire. I have often heard people complain that after reading spiritual books or going to workshops or starting a spiritual practice, they have to replace their televisions, toasters or light bulbs!

Later, as power becomes expensive and scarce, there will be blackouts and electricity cuts in many places. We will learn to co-operate and share resources, allowing buildings like hospitals to take priority.

~ Oil and Gas ~

Available sources of oil and gas will have run out by 2012. There will still be supplies under the seas but these are required for the lubrication of the tectonic plates. The Universal Angel Joules, who is in charge of the oceans will not allow this to happen.

I have received e-mails from people sending me information about oil, which can still be accessed after 2012. However, my guide reiterates the above. We will be living on reserves.

As oil stores dwindle travel will be more expensive and towns will build cycle paths. It will be safer and easier to cycle from place to place. Gas guzzling cars will not be viable and ecological forms of powering vehicles will be developed. More people will travel by public transport, especially by boat and train.

By 2032 fewer people will fly by aeroplane. However, soon after 2032 there will be fast clean ecological methods of transport available that we cannot yet contemplate.

~ Sources of Eco-Energy ~

As a world we will seek natural forms of power, harnessing that from water, lightning, sun and wind. Naturally we will burn coal and wood but the increasing understanding that these are finite resources and the realization of the importance of trees will make this less acceptable. We have become used to using plastic and oil based materials for just about everything. Already many countries are cutting down on the use of polythene bags but this is just a drop in the ocean. We will get used to old-fashioned ways of handling and constructing many things, until we develop new and ecological methods.

More technologists will unconsciously and consciously work with the angels and other high beings to bring forward new forms of ecological power. These will include crystals, earth magnetism, pyramid power and plant energy amongst others.

We will eventually be able to harness energy from the oceans for the use of everyone on the planet but this depends on international peace before it can be developed.

And by 2032 we will be more in charge of the weather, in particular rainfall. For this too we need much higher consciousness and international co-operation and friendship.

As people will live in smaller communities, life will be much simpler and we will value the limited resources of the planet. This change in consciousness will allow the new to come in. Soon after 2032, if it has risen as anticipated we will be able to use sources of power that are currently beyond our understanding and will not harm our planet in any way.

~ Nuclear Power ~

Nuclear power stations will continue to be built and there may be accidents. It is appropriate to hold everyone connected with them in the light.

~ Travel ~

People have always wanted to travel. The desire to expand their horizons by visiting other parts of the world is inbuilt into many souls. However, the fast forms of transport will be less available and former more adventurous types of travel will once more be used. Trains and boats, bicycles and walking will become popular forms of locomotion once more. On one hand travel will be easier as international boundaries will become much looser. On the other, lack of fuel will limit travel until the new begins in 2032.

~ Travel after 2032 ~

Soon after this, individuals will be able to travel with their own little mini-helicopters. Distances will be covered at huge speed in big flying and hovering transport vessels. People will laugh at the old-fashioned internal combustion engine.

My aunt was born in 1911 and lived for nearly ninety years.
She told me that as a child she travelled in a horse and carriage.
In her life she was transported by bicycle, car and jet plane.
She saw space rockets on television taking aeronauts into the
unknown. From horse to space rockets in one hundred years will
seem insignificant in comparison with the advances in methods
of travel in the next twenty-five years!

EXERCISE: *Pay Attention to What you Consume*

For twenty-four hours pay even more attention than usual to the planetary resources that you use, and constantly bless and give thanks for them all. For example, be aware of the electricity you are consuming, notice where the food you purchase has come from and watch the amount of water you use.

CHAPTER 13

The Cleansing of the Planet

PERIODICALLY THROUGHOUT HISTORY parts of the planet have been purged of negative energy, when something new and of higher frequency was to evolve there. The purest places are always those where there has been ice and snow for a long time. Before Golden Atlantis emerged, there was an ice age, which purified the land. It is forecast that another ice age will occur in about 300 years.

Based on the current consciousness, by 2017 Mother Earth will start a major programme of detoxification, throwing off negativity created by the physical and emotional poisons we humans have dumped into her.

Between 2012 and 2032 all the dark places on the entire planet are to be cleansed, and Earth can then raise its frequency and ascend to take its rightful place in the universe once more. The more light we humans bring through us into the Earth, the less purification will be needed. We have the power to change all the possibilities into a gentle transition.

Water has cosmic cleansing properties and was chosen to wash New Orleans where the Earth itself holds the pain, anger and fear of slavery. In this case the flood in August 2005 was also a reminder that all are equal in the eyes of God.

Where cleansing takes place we will regard the destruction with human eyes as horrific. But it will open the hearts of all.

People will start to see their common humanity rather than their cultural differences.

Previously warring countries will be filled with compassion for their neighbours and offer help for the greater good. International boundaries will be relaxed as people co-operate and learn to understand each other.

The tsunami in the Indian Ocean, was also a major piece of purification and in *Angel Answers* I discuss how the Intergalactic Council started planning this well in advance. A cosmic invitation was broadcast throughout the universes for souls to incarnate on a cleansing and healing mission on Earth. Thousands who recognized the great opportunity for service and spiritual promotion responded to the call. Naturally, as soon as they incarnated and went through the veil of amnesia, they forgot their purpose but, at the predestined time of 26 December 2004, they gathered in specific places. These special souls agreed to soak up into their energy fields the negativity of lust, greed, power struggle, poverty consciousness and so on held within the Earth. And on that day the tsunami bore them all into the light together, carrying the toxins with them. Each received a spiritual reward. Only those who had at a soul level agreed to pass over in the 'catastrophe' did so and there were millions of angels waiting to welcome them home with great joy and delight.

As with all major disasters, the watching world opened their hearts with compassion, love, empathy and a desire to help. Those whose lives were turned upside down when they lost loved ones or their livelihood or home, learnt lessons, repaid karma or were offered an opportunity to develop courage, selflessness, co-operation, caring and a hundred other higher qualities.

It is helpful to understand the spiritual perspective but it does not mitigate the grief and loss that may be experienced. The heartfelt prayers of the masses throughout the world in response to the traumas will draw forth assistance, comfort and intercession from the divine realms. And as Earth undergoes its healing crisis, we need to pray constantly for the planet, nature, the animal kingdom and all the people here.

The incidence of natural disasters is expected to continue and intensify especially between 2017 and 2022. They will happen in the anticipated places but also in many unexpected ones. The cleansing will be worldwide.

Mother Earth will use earthquakes, floods, fires, volcanoes, hurricanes and other weather conditions to cleanse and draw attention to systems that need to be changed. Even an epidemic can be utilized for clearing, where the sick people absorb the energy of the disease as well as some of the fear of the area. Those who have a soul contract to pass over into the light take the negativity with them to the higher realms for transmutation.

If enough people have awakened their twelve chakras so that Source energy pours through them into the Earth to heal it, less cleansing by the forces of nature will be necessary. You can also help the healing of the planet by working with the elementals.

Out of the ashes of the old a new way of being will arise like a golden phoenix.

~ How do you Ensure that you are in the Right Place when Cleansing Occurs? ~

Archangel Metatron, the mightiest of the angels, has undertaken the task of ensuring that everyone is in their pre-destined place during the changes.

Some individuals, families, communities or soul groups may have decided to pass over together, like butterflies emerging from their cocoon into the light. Metatron will assist them to be in the right place for this to happen.

Only those who are afraid of death or do not understand the joy of being in the light or can only see this from a human attitude may resist this. The angels assure us there is nothing to fear.

A friend of mine in her late eighties has seen many in her age group and younger die. She always says to their relatives, 'Lucky them. Poor you!' She is highly evolved and recognizes that while on Earth we are like birds in a cage. It is when our spirit is released at death that we are truly free.

If your soul has undertaken that you will remain in your physical body to help others or to continue your experience, then Archangel Metatron will guide you. It is helpful to listen to his promptings!

Just reading this paragraph will help you to attune to him.

You can pray that you are able to follow your guidance to be in the right place at the right time or you can actively connect to Archangel Metatron to assist you to hear his message. The more often you practise this, the stronger your connection will become, even though you may be unconscious of it.

EXERCISE: *Connecting to Archangel Metatron*

1. Find a place where you can be quiet and undisturbed.
2. Sit quietly with palms up in a receptive position.
3. Breathe in a beautiful orange light, Metatron's colour, and on the outbreath sense your aura filling with this energy.
4. Relax as you visualize orange light glowing around you.
5. Invoke Metatron with the words. 'I now invoke the mighty Metatron to connect with me and touch me with his light.'
6. Be quiet and still. You may receive a touch, impression, special thoughts or whispers or you may simply feel calm.
7. When you feel the time is right, thank Archangel Metatron and open your eyes.

CHAPTER 14

Weather Changes Worldwide

THROUGHOUT THE WORLD the weather patterns are changing and this will become more marked after 2012. Between 2017 and 2022 the worldwide weather is forecast to be unstable coinciding with more earthquakes and floods. After 2022 the disasters will stop and there will be calm. Collectively we have the power to change the forecasts. If enough people bring in the light, together we can turn a hurricane into a breeze.

~ Europe ~

If the current consciousness continues, there will be much flooding in Europe; mostly where the land is low and flooding is already widely expected. Unless the people who live there make determined efforts to raise their frequency and bring healing light down through them, most of these places will be under water by 2022. However, areas that have never flooded will be vulnerable as the purification continues.

There will also be earthquakes and more – particularly volcanoes – occurring in unexpected places. In addition, some gales, hurricanes and worse forest fires than we have previously experienced will arise.

~ Australia ~

In strange juxtaposition parts of Australia will become much hotter and parts will be flooded. There will be huge areas that are uninhabitable – more than there are at present but this will all change after 2027.

~ The Indian Continent ~

There has always been flooding in parts of the Indian continent and this will continue and get worse.

~ Africa ~

As in Europe there will be expected and unexpected floods, volcanoes, gales and forest fires. Weather will become more extreme here as elsewhere.

~ Russia ~

A lot of snow will be melting in the vast cold regions and this will result in flooding.

~ Israel, Iraq and Iran ~

There is much clearing to do in these countries as in all war-torn areas of the world. Earthquakes will occur as Mother Earth releases the energy of cruelty and inhumanity. This will help to open the leaders up to compassion and understanding. Iraq is particularly dark and there could be major devastation unless enough people evolve to heal the land and hold the country in the light.

~ China and Japan ~

Both these countries can expect cleansing through earthquakes and floods.

~ Next Ice Age ~

Another ice age will cover the planet in approximately 300 years in order to purify it to a higher level again.

~ Polar Shift ~

This is not expected within the next 100 years.

EXERCISE: *Weather Visualization*

Have you ever sat outside on a dull, cloudy, rainy day and visualized a patch of blue sky appearing, then the sun coming out? Or intensely focused on a cloud forming and rain falling? And it happens. These are the powers of the mind we all have.

As weather becomes more extreme everywhere it will be helpful if people do this for the highest good.

You can do this inside or outside, just as long as you relax your body but focus your mind. Do it if you hear of drought in a part of the world where people are desperate for rain to water their crops or to help dry up floods.

1. Sit quietly and relax your whole body, breathing into any parts that are tense.
2. Imagine a soft white violet light filling your mind.
3. Think of the place that you want to focus on.
4. Then as vividly and clearly as possible imagine blue sky appearing which sizzles up the flood or a black cloud forming from which rain falls onto the fields or gardens.
5. When you have finished thank the angels for bringing this about for the highest good of all. By doing this you are offering an act of grace.
6. Open your eyes.

CHAPTER 15

Forecasts for Asia

~ Afghanistan ~

Western troops will be out of Afghanistan by 2012 but there will still be big problems within the country. However, when this country comes into its true soul energy it will be amazing. It will be moving towards peace by 2032.

The mountains of Afghanistan have long been known for deposits of high quality lapis lazuli, a stone that holds ancient wisdom and is connected to the third eye. Magnificent emeralds are also found here; they are the concretized energy of Archangel Raphael, who is bringing forward abundance, healing and the clearing of the third eye. Many other crystals and gems are embedded in the rocks of Afghanistan. These are maintaining the frequency of the country, so that when it finally awakens a Golden City will emerge here.

Afghanistan is the third eye chakra of the planet, which is the all-seeing eye of enlightenment. As more people become enlightened this will help to bring wisdom and peace to this country. Eventually Afghanistan will play a big role in bringing the light to the whole world.

I have a personal story about Afghanistan for I was born in Pakistan and when my mother was six months pregnant with me, she, my father and a friend decided to take a day trip down the Khyber Pass, the link between Pakistan and Afghanistan. It was known for its magnificence and beauty but even then it was a dangerous place to visit. It was said the local tribes murdered anyone found on the Pass after dark.

Unfortunately the mountains proved too much for my parent's little car and the fuel pump decided to pack in just

as dusk was gathering. In this desperate situation my mother,
being the shortest, had to lie on the half open bonnet on her
stomach, squashing me, and operate the pump by hand all
the way home. I always felt I had a link with Afghanistan!

~ China ~

By 2032 it is expected that China will have changed profoundly. The earthquake of 2008 made it possible for them to accept help from the rest of the world. It also opened the hearts of the Chinese people collectively to the families of the bereaved. And over the next twenty years there will be massive transformation, much of it prompted by tragedy as the country is ravaged by more natural disasters.

Because Eastern and Western cultures are so very different the Chinese believe they are spiritual while the West is not. As the twenty-year period progresses, like the rest of the world the West will experience trauma, which will cause people to work together rather than being driven by a desire for power and material wealth. Then the East will start to see the West as spiritual.

A large percentage of the Chinese population will begin to see spirits and angels, so they will start to ask questions. It will be difficult for even the most diehard sceptics to deny the presence of spirit when they can see and communicate with them.

This will open their right brain, their creative, intuitive, expansive and spiritual aspect and will offer each individual the possibility of making their own personal connection with Source. As a nation, their entire way of thinking about life will transform.

Currently there are many powerful portals and sacred sites, which are not activated. As the people awaken spiritually these places will re-ignite and the portals will open. The light coming through them will touch the hearts and open the transcendent chakras of the masses. It will have an enormous impact on the country as a whole.

Within twenty years the generals will go and be replaced by a system, which my guide Kumeka calls 'Community Love'. Each community will be autonomous and governed with integrity and for the highest good by the local leaders. People will feel safe.

There will be much more freedom for the masses who will learn to honour the divine feminine. This will result in them respecting and honouring girls.

As the people feel more in tune with their world, safer and trusting, they will be ready to stand up for their rights and at the same time share and co-operate with each other. They will treat all animals, especially dogs in a more loving way and begin to value them as evolved souls on their own pathway.

Once more the divine feminine influence of Quan Yin will be felt and China, like Japan, will understand all the elementals, especially the dragons, again. After 2032 when higher energies once more flood the planet the Chinese people will open to their true wisdom and the vast country will be filled with light.

~ Japan ~

Japan, like China, believes the West to be unspiritual and will change their views as the whole world works together in the face of natural disasters. The Japanese too will open their hearts and expand their consciousness to embrace a wider universe.

Japan, China and much of the East had a very strong connection with dragon energy. Dragons are fourth-dimensional elementals that can help us tremendously if we are open to them. As changes take place in their world, the people in Japan will reconnect with the dragon elementals once more, and this will help them to rise above their problems and open up to higher spiritual dimensions. At the same time the divine feminine influence of Quan Yin will enfold the people, just as it did in former times.

~ India ~

Progress here is forecast to be slow but there will be peace within the next twenty years. Currently India has lost its soul and because of this its people have become physically and materially impoverished. When they find their spiritual connection again they will attract in abundance once more. Women will then be honoured, the caste system will dissolve and India and its people will glow with light again.

Many souls from Sirius have incarnated in India over the last twenty years. They bring with them much technological knowledge and minds that are open to new and higher ways of creating things. As the frequency of this country slowly rises, they will be accessing much of the higher scientific information to take the world forward. Many of these scientists will become travelling teachers, helping to spread new understandings at a time when travel will be more difficult.

There is a huge portal at Agra, on which the Taj Mahal was built. This is the Soul Star Chakra of the planet and resonates with the number 11, which means bringing in energy to start again at a higher level. When this opens in 2012 it will have a massive effect on the consciousness of the people.

~ Pakistan ~

I was born in the Himalayas in Pakistan and love the place and its people. But the whole country needs cleansing for there are too many power-hungry people here. When India finds its soul, there will be an impact on Pakistan too and by 2032 the country will be moving towards peace.

~ Tibet ~

Tibet will be free and independent from China by 2022. China will hold on as long as possible but the people will no longer want to keep Tibet in their thrall. By 2032 Tibet will once again be a beacon of light but the Tibetans will no longer want to contain the light within their own country. They will be ready to spread it. Through forgiveness and spiritual practises they will have cleansed the land of the darkness of the tyranny they have experienced.

EXERCISE: *Sending Light to a Country or Place*

You can do this for any country:

1. Find a place where you can be quiet and undisturbed.
2. Light a candle and dedicate it for the highest good of the country you have chosen.
3. Ask the angels of love to go there and fill the place with love and light.
4. Ask that the citizens be happy, laughing, free and prosperous.
5. Blow out the candle and know that the angels are taking the energy to help the people there.

CHAPTER 16

Forecasts for Africa

THERE IS A LOT OF dark energy in Africa. In the northeast of the country this energy is contained deep within the land itself. At the time of Lemuria, certain Africans in these areas practised a version of witch-craft. They were engaged in power struggles with evil intent and this negative energy entered the very earth. It is the fear of witchcraft that is held within the soil, rocks and crystals. There is also fear of change because there might be retribution. It is this, which underlies the violence in Africa. It also affected the pure Lemurians who were connected with that part of the world – and they withdrew.

The Earth itself programmed the crystals within it with dark energy, because it held the energy of the Africans of that time.

And it is from within Africa that the healing and purification can now take place. By programming and directing Lemurian healing crystals to purify the dark crystals in Africa big changes can take place. Healing crystals or healing thoughts can also be focussed on that continent from other parts of the world.

Lemurian healing crystals need to be taken to Egypt too. Then a new grid of light can be set up, allowing Africa to take her true place in the world.

As the consciousness rises Africans will start to demonstrate maturity and wisdom. Corruption will be a thing of the past and honest, high frequency people will step forward in the future to show the way. They will be a living example that true power comes from self-worth and the capacity to empower others.

As the masses find their own self-respect and worth, both men and women will take responsibility for their way of living. The general frequency will rise and they will move towards enlightenment and ascension, automatically drawing higher energies through themselves. This will bring healing and end the AIDS epidemic but not until about 2027.

African people have huge generous hearts and they will forgive the many iniquities, which have been perpetrated on them over the centuries. They will also embrace all those from other cultures who have settled in Africa and made their home there. Africa will blossom into a land of peace and plenty.

The great two-way interdimensional portal at Great Zimbabwe will wake up and become fully operational. It will bring in huge light, which will affect the country considerably.

The portal of Table Mountain will also open completely and its influence will enable Africa to become totally self-sufficient. Hunger will be a horror of the past. These wonderful portals will bring in pure energy and allow higher beings to enter, but they will not bring in Christ consciousness or access help from other planets like the cosmic ones.

Most importantly, the whole of South Africa is the spiritual Solar Plexus chakra of the planet and is currently holding much fear for the world. As the portals open and are activated again, starting in 2012, the anxiety will dissolve and the ancient wisdom will return. As South Africa is connected to Mercury, the planet of communication, this country will be instrumental in spreading golden truth.

~ Egypt ~

Archangel Metatron's retreat is at Luxor in Egypt. He is holding the ascension energy for the planet and brings great light into Egypt.

At the fall of Atlantis, Ra led his tribe to Egypt and they began the Egyptian culture, bringing forward the Pharaohs.

Ra's tribe brought with them the design of the pyramids, which are awesome cosmic computers and help to hold the Earth in alignment with the stars.

The energy of the Sphinx has been on Earth forever and Ra also took this from Atlantis to Egypt. The statue of the Sphinx was constructed to represent that energy. It is connected to Mars, protects and watches over our planet and holds the akashic records at a fifth-dimensional level. This will be released when enough people have raised their frequency to match it.

In 2012 the Nile will flood in an unprecedented way finally cleansing the fear held in the land. We are sent large numbers of photographs taken in Egypt and most of them contain Orbs of stuck souls unable to pass over. Some of these have been hanging around in Egypt for a long time, since the era of the Pharaohs, and have been holding the country back. Once these souls have reached the light the whole area will feel clearer and more peaceful.

As people open their twelve chakras and bring Source light down through their energy system into the Earth, they will energize the ley-lines. In turn this will allow the higher light to flow to the pyramids and energize them. The light will surge through the pyramids and into the universe, helping to draw Earth into the correct alignment for the ascension of the planet. It will also enable Earth to take her rightful place in the universe. So Egypt is very important for the future of our planet.

In addition the incredible portal of the Sphinx will open and have a monumental impact on the Middle East and Africa, ultimately embracing the whole world.

There will be a huge shift in Egypt in 2012 and the mass of the population will open up. This will lead to some confusion and challenges but eventually these souls will see a wider spiritual perspective and will help to raise the light of Africa as well as the Middle East.

EXERCISE: *Sending Healing to Africa*

1. Draw a picture of Africa. It does not have to be accurate, your intention is more important.
2. Draw a line to represent golden wisdom from the top to the bottom.
3. Then colour the rest of the map pink while sending love from your heart into that continent.
4. Outline your map in blue for healing.
5. Know that your focus and energy have made a difference.

CHAPTER 17

Forecasts for the Arctic, Canada and the USA

~ The Arctic ~

This area, like the Antarctic has been covered in snow and ice for a long time, and has therefore been purified. The Innuit, who originated from Golden Atlantis, live here and hold the wisdom of their tribe from that special era.

Because it is a high frequency area it will attract evolved people who will migrate here when it eventually becomes habitable, so that they can bring forward the blueprint for the fifth-dimensional world.

The Arctic is the Stellar Gateway Chakra of the planet and is linked to an energy cluster in the Pleiades, which is in turn connected to a wormhole that has access to Source. The highest and purest light, including the Christ energy, will pour in here when the great portal of the Arctic opens in 2012. It is so huge that it will influence the entire world.

~ Canada ~

Archangel Michael's retreat is at Lake Louise, Banff, and he has been holding the energy of Canada, giving the inhabitants much strength, courage and protection.

With little karma and many older souls incarnating here, this country has been cleansed by ice and snow over a long period of time. The transition years here will be relatively easy and then its light will truly shine and it will help its neighbour, America, to move into ascension.

~ The United States of America ~

Barak Obama became the 44th President of the U.S. in November 2008, in a worldwide wave of excitement that pushed Earth onto her ascension pathway. He is a man of good intent who is instigating moves towards international peace. However, there is a huge backlog of karma in the U.S. as well as resistance against progressive change. The gun lobby is one example, as is the volume of third-dimensional dogmatic souls in the Bible belt.

Deep in the American psyche is a belief that they are special. This has caused them to become remote and isolated from the rest of the world. During the coming changes and purification they will learn to ask for help before they move into a higher consciousness. In addition, as the light comes in waking the masses up psychically and spiritually, the people will start to see spirits and angels. Some will be very shaken as their long cherished beliefs are dashed. It will cause them to question and they will be transformed from a religious country to a spiritual one. The U.S. will ultimately become an open, caring fifth-dimensional nation.

Also as many move spontaneously from the vulnerable places that are flooded and cleansed in other ways to higher parts of the continent they will be affected by the pure energy there and this will enable them to rise in consciousness.

Barak Obama's election is the first step towards the vision of a world where everyone lives in peace, harmony and co-operation.

You can help by doing this visualization. And remember that as the U.S. is so big and powerful, this imaging will help the whole world, not just America.

EXERCISE: *Sending Healing to the USA*

1. Light a candle and dedicate it to the president of the United States, visualizing whoever is holding that office, being connected to the Christ Light.
2. Visualize Lord Meitreya, who holds the Christ light, pouring that golden energy down onto Barak Obama, or any future president.
3. Picture it going down through the president's crown chakra into his heart.

4. Ask the unicorns to help and see them surrounding him and showering him with light from their horns.
5. Visualize Archangel Gabriel purifying the White House.
6. Give thanks to the archangels for their help and open your eyes.

CHAPTER 18

Forecasts for
South America

AT THE END OF ATLANTIS the kundalini or spiritual life force of the planet was taken to the Himalayas where it was held by Sanat Kumara in his retreat in the Gobi Desert. It was a masculine energy.

This energy has now been moved to South America, where it has transformed into a ball of feminine energy and is held by Archangel Sandalphon in his retreat in the Magical Crystal Caves, in Guatemala at the beautiful Lake Atatlan. This energy will be released when the kundalini of the planet rises in 2012. Then South America will flower.

We currently have access to only a fraction of the Mayan wisdom. When it is all accessible again to everyone, South America and the whole world will be enriched by it. It will be a land of happiness and abundance. All the countries of South America will blossom.

~ Peru ~

The whole of Peru is a portal that will open in 2012 to release and radiate the Inca wisdom, which was brought here by Thoth at the fall of Atlantis.

Within the great portal is held one of the four two-way interdimensional portals on the planet, Machu Picchu. The priests thought they had left it protected when they ascended but the explorer Bingham pillaged all the protecting artefacts when he found it. Because of this, darkness was able to enter the planet. Lightworkers have made huge efforts to send light and protection to this portal and it is becoming clearer.

While Lima is very dark and will need to be cleansed, the Andes Mountains are a belt of pure energy. The trees that cover the area also keep the energy held as high as possible for they contain ancient wisdom. From here elementals send out telepathic messages of support and encouragement to their fellow elementals and the tree network.

Commander Ashtar uses this portal to access Earth with his space ships in order to help and protect us.

The angels of communication also come through here bringing the crop circles with their symbols to wake us up.

Peru will ultimately be a country of great light and compassion.

~ Mexico ~

The people of Mexico hold a feeling of unworthiness and guilt within their collective consciousness and fear within the land, which is why the Unites States has resisted them so strongly. This will be cleansed.

There is also much wisdom held within the land. Local portals are starting to awaken, affecting the people and bringing forward ancient wisdom.

In addition, when the portals of Sedona, Arizona and Hawaii open, this will profoundly affect the consciousness of Mexicans and their neighbours.

By 2032 this will be a glorious place to be.

EXERCISE: *Sending Healing to South America*

1. Sit quietly where you will be undisturbed.
2. Light a candle and play soft music if possible.
3. Picture South America in your mind's eye, covered in a carpet of flowers in bud.
4. Visualize the flowers throughout the continent opening up and radiating out light.
5. See people throughout the area dancing, radiant with joy, hand in hand with angels.
6. Know that as you see the flowers opening and the people dancing with angels, this is symbolically opening you up too to love, happiness, spiritual joy and angelic connections.
7. Thank the angels, then open your eyes.

CHAPTER 19

Forecasts for Mongolia and Russia

CURRENTLY THE HEARTS of the people, especially the politicians, are closed with fear of the West. They need to bring the light back and this will happen by 2032 if enough individuals offer their prayers for it to do so.

The new energy coming in will open many up psychically so that they will see things in a very different way, and it will give them hope again. Several major portals are asleep and they will all open in 2012 or soon after, bringing in a huge spiritual awakening for the people. The confidence of the masses will rise and with it their abundance consciousness so they will attract good fortune to their countries. The vast landmass will divide into smaller communities who will live in harmony internally and be at peace with their neighbours.

As in other countries wide-scale flooding will bring the highest out in the people. They will work hard to help their compatriots, and even open up to receive help from elsewhere. Where the snow melts, the land will be pure, so it will attract high frequency newcomers to create fifth-dimensional communities. Eventually Golden Cities will arise here and people will laugh again.

EXERCISE: *Sending Healing to Mongolia and Russia*

1. Sit quietly where you can be undisturbed.
2. Close your eyes and relax by focussing on your breath.
3. Open your heart until you can feel love pouring from it.
4. Send it to any part of the country you feel drawn to.
5. Call in Archangel Gabriel and sense his presence near you.
6. Visualize pure white droplets, like snow floating down over the

area you are focussing on. This is Archangel Gabriel's energy purifying the place.

7. Imagine this white purifying snow falling on land where it has never
been seen before, cleansing and lighting it up.

8. Thank Archangel Gabriel for helping you to purify that country.

CHAPTER 20

Forecasts for Australasia and the Pacific Islands

This is one of the areas most influenced by the Lemurians during their time on the planet, in the times before Atlantis.

~ Australia ~

Contrasting weather conditions will take place in Australia, during the transition. Floods, fires and unprecedented heat waves will create drama in the cleansing period, when more of the land will be uninhabitable.

As the frequency of the planet rises and scientists are allowed to 'discover' the secrets of controlling weather and creating rain, some parts of Australia will become not just habitable but pleasant and beautiful. Once the world has learnt how to bring forward the element of water and can provide it where it is needed, there will be a massive drive towards reforestation and Australia will change beyond recognition.

Despite the way that the English settlers treated the Aborigine natives, there is not too much karma for this country to clear. This is in part due to the way the Aborigines honoured the land for centuries as that accumulated positive energy there. Also, thanks to the climate many people have focussed on sport and outdoor life rather than the greedy accumulation of money and power. Where they have done the latter, the Earth will be cleansed.

~ Uluru ~

The Universal Angel Roquiel has her retreat over Uluru and is holding the energy of Australia.

Uluru is a huge interdimensional portal and it will wake up soon after 2012. This area will become the main welcome portal for space ships and beings to this universe, bringing huge benefits to this area of the world. Many star children from other planets or universes, who understand the importance of intergalactic travel and communication, will incarnate here.

The Australians will bring forward technology provided by the extra terrestrials. In accordance with fifth-dimensional principles they will share all knowledge freely throughout the world. This will be done both by distance telepathy and advanced computer knowledge that we would currently find inconceivable.

In addition when the portal in Hawaii containing the Great Crystal of Lemuria wakens, this will influence Australia immensely, raising the frequency and making the people more gentle. They will become much more in touch with the Earth and want to heal it.

~ New Zealand ~

New Zealand's energy is relatively pristine and the people will all start to work together, co-operating for the highest good.

At the fall of Atlantis one of the twelve tribes led by the High Priestess Hera went to the Pacific Islands and then on to New Zealand. They became the Maori, bringing with them mystical and shamanic knowledge as well as unique farming knowledge which after 2012 will return to the consciousness of the people and help them with the future.

As more people become psychic they will be aware that this country is already an entry portal for space ships of light, especially those of Commander Ashtar's command, which enter here. They will embrace and welcome the presence of light beings from other planets and the help they bring. As a result of the extra assistance it will receive New Zealand will prosper and be an example to the world, especially after the cleansing.

While I was in New Zealand on holiday I was awed to see not only small spacecraft like discs, but also a vast mother ship. To me it looked like a gigantic oval-shaped liner, with portholes ablaze with light. I only saw it for a moment but it is something I will never forget.

~ The Pacific Islands ~

Fiji and Honolulu are the spiritual sacral and navel chakras of the planet. I was fascinated to discover that the early people on another of the Pacific Islands, Easter Island, called that the navel of the world!

These islands express sensuality, warmth and welcome. When the portal opens on Fiji in 2012 the Pacific as a whole will radiate pure love and spread it everywhere. By 2032 a knowing of transcendent sexuality will spread and then AIDS and other sexually transmitted diseases will decline.

At the fall of Atlantis the High Priest Hermes took his tribe to Hawaii, where they became the Kahunas. They brought the powerful dolphin link with them. There is wonderful energy in Hawaii as it contains wisdom from Lemuria as well as Atlantis. The portal here is opening in 2012. As the Great Crystal of Lemuria is held here, this will spread Lemurian wisdom and healing like rays of light round the world.

EXERCISE: *Dolphin Visualization*

1. Find a place where you can be quiet and undisturbed.
2. Ask a dolphin to come to you and spend a few moments experiencing its love and wisdom.
3. Picture huge columns of golden light rising up from Hawaii and Fiji and falling like a fountain over the Pacific.
4. Then be aware of thousands of dolphins taking this golden light to every ocean of the world.
5. When the seas are filled with this golden light, see it rising like a mist and spreading over the landmasses.
6. Focus on barriers dissolving everywhere as people welcome and embrace each other.
7. Thank the dolphins for their energy and open your eyes.

Forecasts for Europe

~ France ~

Because much of France is rural, the greed and corruption mainly found in cities has been contained. Those people who live a simpler life-style will find the transition years easier than those who are in cities, especially as they are already self-sufficient.

The new portal opening in 2012 in the seas by Marseilles will massively change the consciousness of the masses, who will become receptive to new spiritual understanding. Those living in the countryside will open their hearts to the town dwellers who are displaced in the cleansing.

Mother Mary is a wondrous Universal Angel, whose retreat is at Lourdes. Her influence will be even more strongly felt here and healing will spread from this area.

This country will start to co-operate with its neighbours, while still keeping its uniqueness.

~ Germany ~

The last of the darkness of the wars must be cleansed from the land, so unexpected weather conditions will occur which will cause the old to be transmuted.

The guilt, which is held in the collective consciousness of Germany, will be totally cleared in 2012. Then Germany can take its place to spearhead the move to enlightenment. Thousands of mature and wise souls have chosen to incarnate here since the second World War, both to help mitigate old karma and to lead this country forward to enlightenment and ascension.

There is much cosmic wisdom held by the trees in the Black Forest and this will help to anchor and maintain the light in Germany during the changes.

Many fifth-dimensional communities will form here, and after 2032 new Golden Cities will arise in this country.

~ Italy and the Vatican ~

Much beauty is held in Italy for so many Renaissance sculptors and artists chose to work here, raising the frequency as much as they could. This has helped to hold Italy in the light.

Organizations like the Mafia will disappear as their vibration will be too low to attract supporters or people to terrorize.

Within the next twenty years the Vatican as well as some churches that hold people down will collapse. With this the stranglehold of the lower aspects of the Roman Catholic religion will loosen. Gradually true spirituality and the true glory of Christ's message will emerge.

~ Spain and Andorra ~

Spain is a vast country, which will see many changes for it has very mixed energies. As the weather becomes more extreme people will move into the mountains. Where gold and other treasures purloined from the Aztecs and Incas are held, there will be cleansing, causing much disbelief and confusion. Also the pain of the Spanish Inquisition is still held in the land, which must be purified.

Andorra too is dark and light but when the portal opens there, the country will find its true soul expression and this will spread through Spain.

~ England ~

England has lost its purpose over the last decade. The soul decision of the country to balance its karma from the days of the British Empire by allowing mass immigration has resulted in confusion, feeling overwhelmed and political misjudgements. Much negativity in London needs to be transmuted, and it is hoped by the Spiritual Hierarchy that the Olympic Games will bring in such light in 2012 that all karma will be dissolved and the land purified.

Much of London will be cleansed by water during the purification.

As London is the spiritual Earth Star Chakra for the planet, this country will ground the higher light for the new world.

Glastonbury, in the West Country is the Spiritual Heart Chakra of the planet and as this opens fully a welcome will radiate from here round the world and out into the universe.

Situated close to here is Avebury, which used to be a main port for craft from all over the universes. Its power has been cut in two by a road but it will awaken and become whole again. Already the surrounding areas are preparing to fulfil their old role again.

Crop circles were placed here because the land had already been energized for them. Some of the crop circle symbols were signals from other star systems. They were also keys, which opened the consciousness of the people.

The extraterrestrials, who are much wiser than we are, will bring light and assistance to the world. By 2022 England will be ready to accept their help and by 2032 this country will be actively co-operating with the light beings from other star systems.

Some of the areas that will be underwater by 2032 will still be holding important energy even though it is not obvious to us at a human level.

~ Scandinavia ~

Much of Scandinavia has already been cleansed by the snow and those parts will shine by 2032. Older, wiser souls are incarnating here who are preparing for the Golden Age. Many of the scientists are already spiritually open, even though they may not be consciously aware of it. This allows Master Hilarion, who is in charge of technology for the Golden Age to connect with them. As the twenty-year period progresses, this will become more evident and those scientists will become consciously aware. Master Hilarion will be working with the angels to download information to many of them, so that they will bring forward ecological and spiritual technology to take us all into the New World.

~ Switzerland ~

In the mountains the energy is very pure, so fifth-dimensional communities will be formed here.

However, there are two things holding Switzerland back. The first is the Large Hadron Collider beneath the Franco-Swiss border near

Geneva. It is the world's largest and highest-energy particle accelerator and already its construction has cracked the Earth's crust.

In 2009 I travelled to Bern from Zurich to give a lecture. The train had broken down, which is unheard of for Switzerland and we had to take a detour via Geneva. Even though this meant we would be late for the presentation, I felt very calm and meditated during most of the journey. When we arrived the talk had been postponed for half an hour while everyone moved to a bigger venue and I arrived in perfect timing. Later I asked my guide, Kumeka, why this had happened and he told me I had to be taken round the area by train to put energy into the land to mitigate the effects of the Large Hadron Collider.

The second is that there is much karma because the Swiss banking system has colluded for many years to allow greedy and sometimes evil people to hide and hold onto their ill-gotten gains. Wealth that has been stolen or accumulated through the disempowerment or slavery of others is dark energy, which will be cleansed by the elements. This must be swept away for the new to arise; so unexpected earthquakes and flooding will cleanse this negativity, unless the people of Switzerland and the world purify it soon. This precept also applies to Liechtenstein and other places that are protecting dark financial energies.

EXERCISE: *Sending Healing to Europe*

1. Find a place where you can be quiet and undisturbed.
2. If you can, light a candle and dedicate it to Europe being filled with peace, abundance, light and love.
3. Close your eyes and relax.
4. Visualize angels of love and unicorns filling the skies over Europe.
5. The angels are singing and the unicorns are pouring light down.
6. The light is touching every person and place like a cleansing shower.
7. See any dark places being purified.
8. Thank the angels and unicorns.
9. Open your eyes.

CHAPTER 22

Forecasts for
the Middle East

~ Iraq ~

Western troops will withdraw by 2012 but this is a very difficult area where turmoil will continue. Fires, floods and earthquakes will cleanse the land. The inhabitants will learn to co-operate with each other for the good of their country and women will have to take an active part. This will enable them to regain their self-respect and become empowered, thus bringing in the divine feminine. The rising consciousness of women will help to loosen the grip of religious dogma and by 2032 the people will be opening to the higher spiritual understandings pouring into the planet.

At the fall of Atlantis the High Priest Apollo led his tribe to this land, which was then known as Mesopotamia. Much deep wisdom is held here and when the portal opens soon after 2012, it will start to lighten up. Then the wisdom of ancient Persia held within the Earth will emerge at a higher level than before.

~ Israel ~

The huge cleansing needed here by earthquake and other means will result in less available land. However, several things will change the situation beyond recognition. The feeling of fear and vulnerability, which underlies their aggression, will be dissolved as they start to become spiritual rather than religious. The old dogma will be replaced by peaceful hearts who seek resolution not conflict.

Because the United States will have problems of its own, there will no longer be support to bolster up Israel's bravado and a new humility will change their attitude.

As other countries in the Middle East suffer their own cleansing crises, the conflicting countries will become helpful neighbours, looking at each other with compassion not fear. Israel will be at peace by 2032.

~ Iran ~

The peoples of this vast country have tried several times to set themselves free but karma has been holding them back, keeping them subjugated. After 2012 when the portal in Mesopotamia, Iraq, opens, this will profoundly affect Iran. The people will feel their souls are liberated again and peace and joy will return here.

~ Saudi Arabia ~

Ancient karma held in the earth will cause problems, so too will more recent karma as so much oil has been removed. Oil is needed for the lubrication of the planet, which will react against the exploitation of its resources. As this country runs out of oil and money ceases to be currency, there will be challenges.

Camels hold much wisdom and will start to telepathically communicate with the people. This will help the Saudi Arabians to find their soul path.

EXERCISE: *Sending Healing to the Middle East*

Ask the angels of love to hold the people of the Middle East in beautiful pink and white bubbles of love. You can do this any time, when you are walking, driving, pausing in your work or with friends. Simply pause for a moment and send out the thought. You may sense the bubbles of love drifting over the landmass.

CHAPTER 23

Fifth-Dimensional Communities

WHERE AREAS HAVE BEEN CLEANSED small fifth-dimensional communities will be formed and here people will live together for the highest good. When I asked about the governing structure of these places, Kumeka was clearly perplexed at my stupidity. He indicated that by 2032 people will be attuned to each other, many communicating telepathically, so there will be no leader, just Oneness.

> *By 2032 words like 'decision' or 'leader' will not be required because the inhabitants will be living harmoniously and mostly telepathically together so choices will evolve automatically for the benefit and satisfaction of all.*

During the twenty-year transition period a tremendous opportunity is being offered to all those souls who are willing to accept it, to live in a co-operative way, working together for the highest good as we build communities for the Golden Age. It is anticipated that individuals and groups will accept this challenge with humility, so that the new will come in without the constraints of ego. And the more prepared we are the more easily we can make the transition.

With the decline in supermarkets and long distance deliveries, self-sufficiency will be the order of the day. Local areas will grow local food. People will learn to cultivate that which is suitable for their climate – and by 2022 this may be different from that which we are used to as the weather becomes more extreme.

There will no longer be pesticides sprayed onto all crops and the food will be healthier. Communities will support each other as they co-operate and experience how to live naturally once more.

Because many people will have opened up spiritually and psychically they will be seeing angels, fairies and other elementals. Gardeners and farmers will be communicating with the elementals who help the plants to grow – and learning from them. People will see with their own psychic eyes the difference it makes to crops when you bless the water.

They will discover the bounty that nature bestows if treated with respect and love.

When I started my vegetable garden I knew nothing about growing them but every day I blessed the ground and then the seeds when I planted them. Every morning I threw open my back door and thanked the angels and elementals for helping me. I humbly asked them to guide me and prompt me when things needed to be done.

It seemed no time before I had a cornucopia of wonderful vegetables filling the patch. I had a blip when I started to write this book. In my old way I focussed entirely on it and shut out the elementals. Within two days there was an infestation of black fly. Then I tuned into the elementals once more and exchanged energy with them. They told me to bless the plants, wash all the black fly eggs off the leaves with soapy water and then as long as I continued to engage with them, they would protect the plants from such pestilence. I humbly followed their instructions. It took hours to wash the plants and every time I went away for a few days the black fly returned and I had to start again.

Most important of all, I felt a sense of peace and fulfilment I had not experienced for years. My Earth Star Chakra developed in this time, allowing me to accelerate my ascension pathway. And this is what will happen worldwide in the new communities.

Kumeka has assured me that when I get the energy right, the elementals will totally protect the plants and vegetables from all pests and marauders. I still have a way to go but I'm learning.

Because everyone is working for the highest good of all in the fifth-dimensional communities, the older generation will once more be honoured and people will listen to their wisdom. With good organic food, cleaner air, pure water, more peace and quiet, higher frequency satellite communication and a good feeling of belonging, senior citizens will once more become healthy, alert, alive and useful – and this will raise the consciousness of all.

A general feeling of contentment, love and happiness will keep people healthier. Much of the deeply entrenched karma that has kept people stuck and often ill will be dissolved. It was this which necessitated the use of medical drugs for survival. Local medical care, with a return to natural medicines, especially herbs, and a healthy attitude will prevail.

Fifth-dimensional communities engender a sense of belonging, caring and co-operation. Open hearted exchange and sharing promotes togetherness, generosity and higher love. Creativity of all sorts is encouraged, as is spirituality and Oneness.

As the veil between the physical and spiritual worlds lifts there will be a feeling of Oneness with animals, plants and fellow humans. People will begin to remember and feel their brotherhood/sisterhood. This will contribute to the success of small communities with a sense of belonging.

Soon after 2032 new golden cities will arise like Phoenix from the ashes.

EXERCISE: *Cities of Light Visualization*

1. Sit quietly for a few moments and relax.
2. Picture the whole world in front of you.
3. As you look at it spots of light are appearing everywhere.
4. These points are shimmering with golden light. Each point of light is linked with a thread of gold.
5. Bless these golden cities of light.
6. Then see the light from these fifth-dimensional cities shining out into the universe.
7. Give thanks for their service and slowly open your eyes again.

CHAPTER 24

Working with Nature

AT LAST humans are starting to recognize the wisdom of the indigenous tribes who worked with and encouraged nature. They honoured the natural world, loved and respected it, with the result that it yielded its generous, abundant bounty and contributed to the health of all people and animals.

The damage most humans have done is enormous. The sooner we all start to listen to the voice of nature and respond to it, the more healing we can do on Earth and the easier our transition into the Golden Age will be.

Those who connect with the nature kingdom during the transition period will receive extraordinary guidance and assistance from the myriad of unseen beings around us. By 2032 everyone within the new fifth-dimensional communities will be very aware of and grateful to its many aspects that we currently ignore.

~ The Nature Kingdom ~

The angel in charge of the whole of the nature kingdom is the Universal Angel Purlimiek, who is a wondrous, luminous pale green blue colour. He co-ordinates with many of the other Universal Angels and Lady Gaia to keep Earth in balance and harmony. He is in charge of the elemental masters and the elementals.

The elemental masters vibrate between the fifth- and sixth-dimensional frequency, while the elementals frequency is mostly of the fourth dimension. Some fairies, goblins and all the tree elementals called warb-urtons are fifth-dimensional. As we raise our frequency and open up psychically and spiritually we will automatically see or sense the millions of creatures who are helping nature to provide for us. When we understand the role of the elementals and the importance of what they do, we will start to co-operate with them. This could have a huge impact on the regeneration of the planet to help us all during the coming decades.

Elementals are nature spirits who look after the different aspects of the natural world. They may be of fire, air, earth, water and, according to Chinese wisdom, wood and metal. They look after the soil, the trees, the plants, help with photosynthesis, cleanse earth, air and water and do a million other jobs to keep the organism of Earth alive. They are light and fun loving.

Recently we have been sent many Orbs of angels carrying an elemental. We have also seen a number of angel Orbs on people's crown chakras with an imp or a pixie inside it. This is to encourage the person to open to his higher self in a happy, light way. Fairies can often be seen in angel Orbs around children, cheering them up and lightening their spirits.

They are called elementals because they do not have the full complement of elements that animals and humans do. Many of them contain one element only and others combine one or more elements.

~ Elementals of One Element Only ~

- AIR - fairies, esaks and sylphs.
- EARTH - pixies, elves, goblins and gnomes.
- WATER - mermaids, kyhils and undines.
- FIRE - salamanders.
- WOOD - warb-urtons

~ Combined Elements ~

- IMPS AND FAUNS contain the combined elements of earth, air and water.
- DRAGONS can be earth, air or fire or a mixture of two or three of these elements.

Just because they contain fewer elements than we do, it does not mean these beings are not evolved. They have simply developed differently from humans. They are of the angelic hierarchy and take their colours from the angels with whom they are connected. Many of the earth elementals are green or green blue, which is a reflection of the ray on which the Universal Angel of Nature, Purlimiek, works.

The colour vibration of flowers is connected to Archangelic energies and the fairies bring those vibrations to the blooms they are tending. For example if a pansy is to be golden yellow the fairies in charge of it blossoming will connect with Archangel Uriel and his deep golden yellow energy. Then anyone seeing those particular pansies will be subtly touched by Archangel Uriel's energy.

The fifth-dimensional fairies are mighty beings, not the naughty creatures we have been taught, though they are light and fun. While the angels, archangels and unicorns are undertaking projects to help the planet, these fairies hold the energy in place. They often continue to do so when the higher beings have finished their work and moved on.

Vegetables have a flower and its colour vibration will ultimately be absorbed into the fruit. For example, a courgette (zucchini) flower is deep yellow, the colour of courage and wisdom, so if you eat one it will affect your subtle bodies with these energies.

Certain elementals are very evolved, like the fifth-dimensional wood elementals, the warb-urtons. Wood holds knowledge from this planet and from the stars and the warb-urtons help to spread it. They are tall, mostly about 4ft (1 metre 20 cms) and they live in trees which have reached a certain size and level of wisdom. When you walk among mature trees, you can be sure that the warb-urtons are trying to communicate with you if you are ready. So try to be quiet and listen to any information they are willing to impart.

When the weather patterns change and Lady Gaia starts cleansing her planet in earnest, there will be much more for the elementals to do. (They are already pretty busy). We humans can help them by appreciating their work, listening to their guidance when we are growing plants and tuning into their wisdom. We can also keep steady and focussed, so that they remain calm.

In difficult times the Angel of Nature, Purlimiek, sends his angels to help the elementals. The angels hold the energy and encourage them to help plants, the soil or the waters.

As an example, fauns who are elementals of earth, air and water, help to balance the energy of forests and woodlands through the process of photosynthesis. As more of our heritage is chopped down they need hope and inspiration, which is provided by many angels. Those humans who understand the elemental world can help too by thanking them and also by sending prayers to uphold them. Walk in the woods and notice what a wonderful effort they are making and this will encourage the fauns. You may even see them dancing in between the trees.

~ New Elementals ~

The Universal Angel Butyalil, who is in charge of the cosmic currents affecting Earth, together with the Angel of Nature, Purlimiek, recently invited several new elementals to our planet to help with its purification. Kyhils are cleansing the waters and esaks are purifying physical and psychic dirt here. Other elementals have arrived to clear woodlands of fear. They all come from other universes and in exchange for their service here they receive an opportunity to experience Earth and to take their learning back to their home planets.

These newcomers to Earth have arrived in the last few years in preparation for 2012 and the major planetary purification, which has already started to take place.

~ Poseidon and the Elemental Masters ~

Working with Universal Angel Purlimiek is the great master Poseidon, the strategist who is planning and managing the cleansing operation. If a storm, hurricane, earthquake or some other form of purification is required, he calls on the appropriate Elemental Master who commands his elementals to take action.

- The Elemental Master of the air is Dom, who orders the sylphs to raise wind.
- The Elemental Master of water is Neptune and he tells the water sprites, mermaids and kyhils to move the waters.
  The Elemental Master of fire is Thor, who invites the salamanders to fan fire.
- The Elemental Master of Earth is Taia, who asks the pixies, elves and gnomes to shift the Earth.

However, if an earthquake is needed to release negativity deep within the Earth, Lady Gaia and Poseidon consult together before they give the orders to the elementals to cleanse an area thoroughly but respectfully. Elementals are very open to the emotional energy of people and when there is a great deal of fear, this whips them into a frenzy, which is when great damage occurs.

Humans have a role in helping to mitigate the impact of some disasters. Your prayers, visualizations, blessings or communication may change the course of events somewhere.

EXERCISE: *What You Can Do to Help*

1. Bless the ground where crystals, coal or anything else has been dug out.
2. Communicate your gratitude to the nature spirits. Just sitting quietly on your lawn, appreciating your garden helps them. Actively thanking and blessing them for their work is even better.
3. If you are gardening, mentally ask the elementals for guidance and then follow your intuition, which is how they communicate with you.
4. Hug a tree and listen to any message it has for you.
5. When weather conditions are inclement, stay calm and soothe everything with pale green-blue light.
6. Grow and buy organic vegetables.
7. Walk on the earth in bare feet. This will also help you ground yourself by connecting more deeply with your Earth Chakra.

CHAPTER 25

Bees

I REMEMBER GOLDEN DAYS, sitting in meadows full of wild flowers, drowsily listening to the buzz of fat yellow-and-black-striped bumble bees and the drone of honey bees as they collected the nectar. Now they are quietly vanishing, abandoning their hives and returning from whence they came.

Bees originate from the Pleiades. They came in the days of Golden Atlantis to learn about the sweetness of life and to serve us by pollinating flowers. They taught us about aspects of sacred geometry and demonstrated an ordered community life with harmonious industry. They were even prepared to share some of their honey with us.

Without bees we cannot survive on Earth. We rely on them to pollinate our plants and trees.

For thousands of years we have exploited these generous, industrious creatures. We have taken their honey, which they produce to keep themselves strong and healthy over the winter months and fed them a poor substitute, polluted their land and moved them constantly. Even worse we have set up satellite broadcasting stations, which confuse them and undermine their resistance. They are deeply stressed, leaving them prey to the varroa destructor mite.

~ What Will Happen to the Bees? ~

It is not too late to change the way we treat them and the planet but it soon may be. We have to raise the conscious awareness of as many people as we can to the plight of bees and many other creatures that are essential for the survival of Earth in its current form.

The most hopeful forecast is that by 2022 there will be a change in attitude worldwide so that pesticides will be discouraged and in many places banned. The severe weather conditions in many places will damage the proliferating satellite stations for mobile phones, computers and other forms of communication. Our attention will be on other matters and they will not all be replaced in the same form. There will be a growing understanding of the needs of bees, dolphins, whales and other advanced life forms and they will be respected.

In that case the bees that survive will once more grow in numbers and in happiness to continue their journey on Earth.

~ So What Can We Do? ~

The glue that makes us all part of the Oneness is love. Your consciousness impacts on and can profoundly affect the physical, emotional, mental and spiritual bodies of all beings. If all people of good intent on the planet took responsibility for their thoughts and emotions, and directed them towards perfect health and well being for all, the consciousness of our world would rise overnight. There would be dramatic changes and our planet would become a congenial place for all, including bees, which would thrive.

You can make a difference. If you sat down for a few minutes each day and envisioned the bees happy, healthy and free, your vision would link with all the other positive pictures and send a message of hope and encouragement to all creatures of the world, not just the bees.

~ How Spiritual Connections Help ~

Our physical third-dimensional world is interpenetrated by beings of other dimensions, many of which look after us. Most people know that a guardian angel holds your divine blueprint and watches over you. You also have an overlighting Archangel who keeps an eye on you, to say nothing of many other angels, unicorns and beings of light who are waiting to help. You can always ask someone's guardian angel to lighten their burden, open doors or care for them in one of many ways. Your prayer then acts as grace and raises the frequency round the person in need, allowing their angel to step closer to them.

~ *Bees and Their Spiritual Connections* ~

All creatures receive spiritual guidance and assistance. The bees work very closely with pixies, who are earth elementals. Pixies look after the structure of the soil and also help the bees to pollinate flowers. In turn imps, who are tiny little 1 inch or 2.5cm tall elementals of combined earth, air and water, work with pixies. On a more cosmic level Lady Gaia is in charge of the earth of the planet and her soul encapsulates Earth. She is one of the highest beings of the angelic hierarchy. She works in harmony with Universal Angel Purlimiek, the angel of nature and they consult with the elemental masters who give commands to the elementals, including the pixies. Every time you send love, encouragement, thanks and kindness to the pixies they will be able to more effectively help the wonderful, life-giving bees. Your gratitude and blessings will touch their souls and help our world.

EXERCISE: *Visualization to Help the Bees*

1. Light a candle.
2. Picture the bees, happy, respected, thriving and swarming back to their hives.
3. Visualize people everywhere truly appreciating them.
4. See the pixies laughing as they help the bees to pollinate the plants throughout the world.
5. Imagine them all bathed in beautiful pink love.
6. Blow out the candle and send the light to the bees and pixies.

CHAPTER 26

Trees

TREES OFFER SO MUCH to our planet and we need to value and appreciate them for their wisdom as well as for the use they have to us.

They are ancient wise beings who keep records of local history and form a network round the planet. Each species of tree has a different quality that it offers to the world. For example, if you wanted qualities of strength and sturdiness, you might intuitively lean against an oak tree. Remember that you can call on ethereal angels and elementals for help but you can also tune into trees for the assistance that you need and you will receive it in a very grounded way.

Large forests are keepers of ancient wisdom. They anchor it and help to hold the energy of the country in which they grow. They even bring in the light from other planetary systems and store it until we are ready for it.

~ Oak ~

Oak trees hold superb, strong, stable and sturdy energy. If you connect with one or sit under it, you will receive these qualities to help you. However they are starting to feel tired because there are now fewer of them to hold wisdom and strength. They need to be re-energized and humans can help to do this by appreciating them.

~ Ash ~

The delicate ash carries divine feminine wisdom and will happily impart this to you when you are ready. They grace many a leyline and help to soften and balance its energy with their gentle splendour.

~ Elm ~

These trees help you to be quick and powerful but also remind you to stay balanced. Currently their numbers are decimated in the United Kingdom and Europe as well as parts of America by Dutch Elm disease. This disease occurred once before, in the 16th century. At that time a massive number of bodies of people who had died of the plague were buried on the leylines. This affected those leylines badly. Because elm trees are sensitive, those along the lines were affected first and this later spread.

When the energy in leylines backs up because of a blockage in the flow, it stops the trees receiving the spiritual and psychic energy that they need. Elm trees are particularly susceptible. In current times, when the English Channel tunnel and the Dartford tunnel were dug out near to each other, it badly disrupted the flow. This is when the elm trees succumbed for a second time to Dutch Elm disease.

It is hoped that the high frequency light coming in will flush out the blockages or re-route the energy, so that the elms can flourish again. And as humans raise their consciousness we will be more aware of the needs of those who are co-sharing the planet.

~ Poplar ~

This fast growing tree is very dependable and teaches you to be dependable too so that others can rely on you.

~ Mahogany ~

This powerful tree radiates magnificence as well as reliability, strength and trust.

~ Beech ~

These beautiful, elegant yet sturdy trees help humans with forgiveness. Lean against a beech tree or visualize one and they will assist you to release hurt, trauma or deception through forgiveness.

~ Holly ~

The dark and prickly holly brings us the lesson: 'Do not judge by outer appearances.' There is a reason why people behave in a hurtful or rejecting way and it is to do with their feelings about themselves, not you. Remember this when you see a holly tree and it will soothe you.

~ Hawthorn ~

These prickly and sometimes scruffy trees offer you protection. They will protect your home and garden and also you as an individual when you are inside that space. They are full of compassion and love but are mighty warriors when it comes to looking after their charges.

~ Chestnut ~

This is the tree that teaches us about abundance consciousness and playfulness. They offer hope and higher expectations, as well as joy and happiness.

~ Plane (Sycamore) ~

The plane trees are very sensitive and they empathize with human vulnerability, offering us protection from our own weakness. As they shelter you, they tune into your feelings and help you to feel better.

~ Silver Birch ~

This tree is very elegant, beautiful and flowing. Its gift is harmony and vulnerability, seemingly opposites, but together they open your heart.

~ Fir and Pine Trees ~

These trees both offer healing, rejuvenation and regeneration. They lift the spirits and purify you. Walking amongst them can restore your health and raise your consciousness to the fifth dimension if you are ready.

EXERCISE: *Visualization to Help Trees*

If you can, do this while standing or sitting under a tree or in woods or a forest. If that is not possible, visualize yourself leaning against a tree.

1. Touch the bark of the tree and through your fingertips feel what it is like. This is its skin or outer protection. Tune into how it feels inside and feel as if you have merged with the tree.
2. What are your roots like and do you feel you are held by them?
3. How sturdy is your trunk? Is the energy flowing freely from the roots?
4. What are your branches like? Do you have space to grow? Are you reaching up or drooping down? How does this feel?
5. Are you in leaf, fruiting, flowering? Sense how this is.
6. Breathe in the qualities the tree is offering you and accept this as a gift.
7. What does the tree need from you? Give it what you can.
8. Thank the tree and draw your energy away from it.
9. Notice how you feel.

CHAPTER 27

Population

NEARLY SEVEN BILLION SOULS have been allowed to incarnate during the end times because of the chance to balance karma and the incredible opportunities for spiritual growth available. The planet is bursting at the seams and this number is not sustainable for long. It would not be allowed if it were not for the extraordinary energies that can be accessed in the next few years. For a planet to move from the third to the fifth dimension in the space of one lifetime has been hitherto unknown. Furthermore Earth is the Everest of all experiences and it takes brave souls to apply to come here. For this reason Source has responded favourably to petitions from beings from all over the universes and agreed that we can all be here now.

The challenges thrown up by the current turmoil are enormous. This will intensify as individuals and communities will have to decide whether or not to open their hearts and include those worse off than themselves or to close their hearts and turn them away.

An early wonderful decision for the light was made by West Germany to embrace the population of East Germany when the Berlin Wall came down. They decided to take in their brothers and sisters, even though it would damage them financially. It was a truly spiritual decision, which has raised the overall vibration of Germany.

China faced a difficult decision as it became too overcrowded to survive. It decreed that couples could have only one child or else they would have burst under the burden of souls entering. This has created an interesting spiritual dilemma, for millions of souls worldwide have connected themselves to a mother, knowing that they would be aborted. Those souls chose that destiny because it offered them an opportunity to experience the Earth changes through the family they had attached to, even though they did not fully incarnate.

And then a divine paradox occurred. Many then became trapped in the aura of Earth. They experienced human emotions, feeling rejected and shocked when they were aborted, with the result that they could not find their way to the light. Currently millions of stuck souls are clogging the energy fields of the planet, especially in countries where abortion is the contraception of choice.

Where an aborted, miscarried or stillborn soul is not acknowledged, it can profoundly impact on the mother and sometimes the father. If parents realized this they would create a little ceremony for the child to help it pass. At the very least they would light a candle for the soul, bless it and help it to reach the light. Once it has done so it can return to learn from the family without drawing on and draining their energy.

After 2032 in the fifth-dimensional communities all babies will be wanted. Parenthood will once more be considered to be the greatest spiritual responsibility an adult can undertake in a lifetime. It will be as it was in Golden Atlantis. If a couple is ready for a baby, they will meditate for the kind of soul they can best serve. Then they will invite one such spirit to connect with them and the act of intercourse will draw him or her to them to be conceived in the mother's womb. The baby will be welcomed and loved by the parents and the entire community.

Once a person has incarnated they cannot die unless their soul and Source agrees. However, in these incredible times the Godhead has determined that millions can pass over, each taking a little of the planet's negativity with them as their service work.

The population is scheduled to drop considerably over the next twenty years. Fewer will choose to be born and many will make choices to move on, often with friends and family, to experience another planet or plane of existence. This is another reason we will once more be living in smaller, co-operative communities.

Because there will be many challenges involved in the forthcoming changes, people will open their hearts and want to help each other. As a result massive international co-operation will take place wherever there are natural disasters. Countries and races will start to understand that the differences are only skin deep. They will begin to honour and respect each other's cultures.

By 2032 there will be a loosening of international boundaries and peace will prevail over much of the planet. We really are moving through the healing crisis into a different world.

EXERCISE: *Helping Stuck Souls to Pass*

This will help to clear the energy fields of Earth and you will need to put on psychic protection because many of the stuck souls are needy and may attach to you. The whole purpose is to point them to the light, not keep them with you!

1. Light a candle and dedicate it to helping many souls to pass.
2. Ask Archangel Michael to place his deep blue cloak of protection over you. Sense or feel it happening and zip it up from under your feet to your chin and then pull the hood up and bring it down over your third eye at the front.
3. Invoke the Gold Ray of Christ to protect you. Do this three times and sense the protective energy forming round you.
4. Mentally form a column of light from you to the heavens. Make this as bright and powerful as you can.
5. Call in Mother Mary and her angels. Ask them to bring stuck souls to the light and help them rise up through the light to the heavens. You can name a particular place or country if you wish to. Lost souls tend to congregate in cities.
6. You may have a sense of people waving goodbye to you as they enter the light. You may even hear them thank you.
7. Invoke Archangel Gabriel to pour his pure white light over and through you to purify you totally and ensure no one has attached to you.
8. Thank Mother Mary, her angels and Archangel Gabriel.
9. You may like to play a singing bowl or other music to cleanse the room.

CHAPTER 28

Children

IT IS FORECAST that by 2032 17% of babies will be born with their 12 strands of DNA active. This figure could be increased if there are enough high frequency adults to birth them and look after them appropriately. As more adults are opening their twelve chakras this may well be possible.

Because these children will be telepathic, clairvoyant, psychic on every level and have extraordinary gifts like the ability to apport, teleport, levitate, communicate with other life forms and heal, their parents must be able to understand and nurture their talents.

In Golden Atlantis each child was taken to the local priest who read their past lives and recognized the individual specialities the soul brought with them. Then their specific abilities were developed by the parents, the community and school, so that the child could do what he loved to do and did best. This was a recipe for happy, contented, fulfilled lives. By 2032 this will start to happen again and most people will feel more soul satisfaction than has been the case for thousands of years. As a planet we will start again to give children what they need rather than what we want for them.

~ Indigo, Crystal and Rainbow Children ~

A wave of souls has already come in from Orion, the plan These are the indigo, crystal and rainbow children, who a lightened. Unfortunately, because of the low frequencies aro many close down to their gifts or withdraw part of their sou and become autistic. Some need space to exercise their energy ture to balance and hold them. As this is denied them, they be hyperactive and often disruptive. They need to be surrounded by vibrations, happiness, beautiful music and fifth-dimensional qualities, nurtured with pure, light food and water and truly loved.

These enlightened children have never experienced any planet other than their home on Orion. They have been prepared by their wise teachers to incarnate on Earth to help bring a wave of enlightenment to us. But nothing can truly make a being ready for such a change in vibration.

The unicorns are trying to help these children and their parents can assist by talking to them about those mighty seventh-dimensional creatures, who are the purest of the pure.

Unicorns have a special empathy with enlightened children, especially those who have difficulties with their incarnation. They help them connect with their original soul intention and to ground it.

As we on Earth raise our frequency it will be easier for those from Orion to live amongst us. So there will be more of these high frequency children coming in during the twenty years after 2012 and they will have a big, positive impact on the consciousness of the planet.

Note not all autistic or difficult children are indigo, crystal or rainbow children!

~ Star Children ~

There are many who are continuing to come to Earth from other universes, stars and planets. They bring many gifts though some are still coming simply to experience life on this plane.

Some of these have not been here before, and even some who have, will not be able to cope with the ethos of current schools. They are seeking peaceful ways of relating. Not only are cultures being mixed up but souls from many different parts of the universes are all intermingling in schools. This has never been honoured in our systems but in the future it will be. New movements will arise which teach them how to understand each other and to relate considerately. This will have a big impact on how children feel. They will have proper tools for expression.

These children need to be active and they will demand space, sport, time in nature and fun. They are very sensitive and attuned to the elemental kingdom. Many have huge compassion, which is another reason they find it so very difficult on Earth. Some are very connected to animals. They have a wealth of insight, feeling and empathy to offer us but many adults will find this hard to relate to.

When their families or teachers link into them at their right vibration then they expand, open their hearts and shine. But because they are so sensitive, if they are misunderstood they can withdraw and close down. Then you never see who they truly are.

It is really important to recognize this and we need to train teachers and light workers to tune into them.

~ Wise Old Souls Being Born ~

Many wise old souls are returning to Earth now to help with the transition between 2012 and 2032. This is a time when communities need to be built up on a fifth-dimensional basis.

Because of the planetary cleansing taking place wise, compassionate souls are needed to comfort those who have lost homes or loved ones. Most importantly they are needed to be beacons that hold the vision of the glorious future for those who are despondent or have lost hope in challenging circumstances.

~ Souls Born through IVF ~

Children born as a result of In Vitro Fertilization (IVF) come from other universes and have never been to Earth before. They come without past life connections to members of their family. They are very special not only because they are so wanted but also because they are totally innocent, brand new to Earth. Because they are so pure and in their essence, they can tune into the needs of the parents and heal them.

With conventional conception there is a surge of emotion as the sperm meets the egg, to become the foetus. This emotion is not there to affect an IVF baby. There is a wave of such souls entering who have the ability to stand back and examine things from a different perspective. Many of them are like a breath of fresh air and will change long accepted things for the better, some on a family level, others on a global one.

While they will have been prepared for their journey on this planet, they may not fully understand it and may need assistance to do so.

I have a friend whose daughter has a much loved and wanted IVF-baby. We may never have met on Earth before but she has a very powerful cosmic connection with me, so we have a strong soul connection. I was due to visit her one afternoon soon after she was born but in the morning I heard her calling me, so I dropped everything and went to greet her with a cuddle.

~ Souls Born after 2012 ~

After 2012 the souls born will have a contract to serve in some capacity. Even if they only live for a few hours they will have agreed to help the planetary transition. They may bring in and anchor a special energy; or they may take some negativity from Earth with them back to the spiritual realms for cleansing; or undertake some other task.

~ Education ~

In many parts of the world children are often considered to be chattels. Often parents expect their children to conform to their ideas and way of life and so they control them. Few truly regard their children as unique souls whose individual talents need to be nurtured. They are handed over to sometimes questionable or immature babysitters and put in schools where they may be bullied, crammed with boring and sometimes wrong information and where their souls are constricted and stultified.

This will change

As the twenty-year period unfolds education will become more suitable for children rather than the adults who administer it. Huge schools built on the model of a business for the ego gratification of the politicians will no longer be considered suitable for the future generations as it dawns on humanity that we need to cherish our offspring. Community schools will replace the old schools and children will flower.

They will be taught less of other people's ideas and their innate gifts will be drawn out more. Education will be right- and left-brain-balanced, with more creative expression and honest communication encouraged. These smaller local schools will allow contented, balanced and evolved children to emerge, ready for the Golden Age.

~ Music ~

Harmonious sounds bring individuals into harmony. In schools music will be played to heal and soothe children so that they can learn more easily.

EXERCISE: *Visualization – Helping Children Everywhere*

1. If you can light a candle and play soft music.
2. Close your eyes and relax.
3. Visualize yourself in a beautiful meadow in the moonlight.
4. Suddenly a great white light appears and a huge, magnificent unicorn stands in front of you. It greets you and invites you to get onto its back. This happens easily and effortlessly. You feel totally safe.
5. Now you are aware of unicorns arriving from all directions, each one carrying a child. Hundred and thousands of children on their unicorns surround you.
6. You, on your unicorn, are leading them through the universe.
7. You arrive at a vast hall of learning on the inner planes.
8. The children remain on their unicorns while a great being of light addresses them telepathically, reminding them of their divine missions on Earth.
9. Special angelic music is played and you can see the fear being lifted from the children's auras and rising like a dark cloud to be transmuted in the light.
10. Archangel Chamuel's angels of love touch every child and their hearts open and shine.
11. Archangel Michael is filling the hall with blue light and this is entering the children's auras.
12. Every child you have taken with you has been touched and helped. Now it is time to return. Again you lead the way back to the meadow.
13. This time you are followed by thousands of lights as the children's hearts radiate like beacons.
14. Back in the meadow, thank them for coming with you. Then receive their roar of thanks to you.
15. Watch them disperse back to where they came from.
16. Dismount from your unicorn. Thank it and watch it disappear, knowing it will come back whenever you need it.
17. Open your eyes, knowing you have done an important piece of service work.

People Power

THE WORLD IS STARTING to see the rise of people power. When individuals worldwide start to accept self-responsibility, they will make their own choices. Everywhere citizens are demanding freedom, honesty, peace and fairness. The old paradigm of leaders and led, rich and poor, authority and submission, adversarial politics or dictatorship, is losing its grip. Already co-creation and co-operation are becoming possibilities.

By 2032 the European parliament will have been swept away. Mugabe of Zimbabwe and the Ayatolla will have long gone and the people will remember with amazement what they endured. The Taliban and the last of the warlords will be disappearing soon after this date. Police states will be challenged everywhere. People will revolt against Big Brother spying, including all suggestions of microchips being implanted.

As the damage done by pharmaceutical drugs and processed foods really reaches the public awareness, people power will ensure that the former gentler healing ways and good food are once more embraced.

The public will demand that the secrets of the Vatican are revealed. Most importantly some of the original Scrolls of the Essenes, the tribe to which Jesus belonged, currently held within the Vatican will be returned to open view. People will see its spiritual emphasis and begin to understand the truth of Mary Magdalene, one of his greatest disciples who carries the divine feminine.

Because all secrets must be revealed, if some are withheld, the building housing the hidden information will be demolished.

There will be an international movement to ban genetically modified products and this will come about by 2022. As the spiritual frequency rises public pressure will result in cloning, some transplants and the use of experiments on animals being outlawed. There will be a grass roots movement back to natural and organic.

Worldwide organized crime will diminish and stop as populations raise their consciousness and a move towards Oneness flows across the planet. The Mafia and the Triads will be names of the old world and by 2032 people will be surprised when they recall their activities. Much of their wealth and influence has been based on the drugs trade. As people become happier, enriched by their spiritual connections and feel they belong in their communities and on Earth, most will no longer turn to addictive supports. Instead their energy will be directed towards co-creating the new communities.

Inevitably there will be a few who cannot cope in the world and will seek mind altering substances as a crutch but their treatment will be very different as natural therapies help them to re-balance their chakras and community love holds them.

In the pre-2012 paradigm the masses gave their power to leaders and with it responsibility for their lives. In the new every individual will be treated as an important contributing part of society.

EXERCISE: *To Take Charge of your own Destiny*

This week notice how you take decisions in every area of your life. Do you defer to others or do you take quick clear ones? Be aware how you take responsibility for your incarnation. If you feel you are a victim or someone else runs your life, decide what you can do to become stronger. You may give power to the government, your doctor, your children, your partner, your boss or any number of people. Be in command and slowly, carefully draw that power to where it belongs.

Affirm: 'I am in charge of my destiny.'

CHAPTER 30

Initiation and Crucifixion

AN INITIATION is a right of passage to a much higher level of evolution. There are seven stages and each soul with the help of the archangels chooses the test it most needs. The tests may be so severe that they involve the life or health of the individual. This means that the person gives something important in order to receive higher gifts of spirit.

The suffering involved acts as a cleanser and purifier at a soul level. Usually the person undertakes something for the collective and so helps many people.

Some people take several initiations in one lifetime. Others spread their journey over many lives. And a soul may choose to retake initiations even though they have done them before in previous incarnations. Remember it is the soul who chooses, not the personality incarnated on Earth.

Because of the opportunities for spiritual growth available now and over the next few years, many souls are undertaking these spiritual challenges. This is one reason why so many people seem to be having such a difficult time. Whole families often agree to go through initiations together. For example one member of the family having a serious operation, an accident, a sick child, losing a job or some other problem, may offer everyone in that group the conditions for their different initiations.

I still remember the horror I felt about John McCarthy being taken at gunpoint and imprisoned in Beirut by the Islamic Jihad. He was held captive in chains for more than five years. When I read his book about it, I couldn't bear it. I shivered with horror all the way through it. I knew he must be going through an initiation but I was more than surprised to learn that this was his first initiation! It felt such an appalling thing to go through.

On the other hand I felt very different about the capture and imprisonment of Brian Keenan and Terry Waite by the same group and later understood that they were both repaying karma.

The first initiation tests the physical body and results in spiritual awakening. The person who has undertaken it is now a spiritual disciple whether he realizes it or not. For some people the actual initiation may be birth itself.

The second initiation involves taking charge of the emotions and is one of the most difficult ones to achieve. Sometimes it takes many lifetimes to master the emotional body and be ready for this challenge. People often think that the tests involved are karmic repayments when the person is really going through a spiritual initiation.

A lady I know whom I will call Annabel fell in love for the first time in her thirties. The man messed her about unmercifully and she had a one-night stand with his friend. She got pregnant and after much agonizing had an abortion. The trauma she went through was her second initiation and all the men involved played their part well in presenting her with the conditions.

Following the physical and emotional challenges comes the third one, the mental initiation. After that the disciple takes mastery of his thoughts and uses them constructively.

A friend of mine, Truda, a bubbly, bouncy, cheerful blonde, is passionate about angels. She is a Reiki Master and helps many people. One day she felt unwell and thought she had flu. A few days later she was getting worse and eventually was rushed to hospital. It transpired that she had a very serious case of blood poisoning and they did not think she could live. At this point she fell asleep and had a classic near-death experience.

She found herself going through a dark tunnel into the brightest light, full of angels. Here she was told she had work to do and must go back.

She was rushed to a different hospital for a life-saving heart operation. We were told they were going to remove a kidney, which was badly infected. Hundreds of people responded and were praying for her and lighting candles. It transpired she was too ill for the surgeon to operate on the kidney as well as her heart, which was a blessing as she never did need to have it removed.

Kumeka told me that she was undertaking her third initiation. Through her physical and mental body she was clearing almost all the ancestral karma of her entire family since time began, which is an almighty undertaking. She was also passing some of the fear from Atlantis through her system.

Truda was desperately ill but she recovered with the help of a new heart valve, a multitude of prayers and massive help from the angels. For example, one day I was sitting quietly by my wood burning stove listening to Gregorian Chants. I lit candles and sat down to focus healing onto her. Suddenly a flash of the brightest and most awesome emerald green passed through me. It was Archangel Raphael taking the opportunity to come through me himself to give her healing. It was awe-inspiring.

I wondered why this was her third initiation, the mental one. Kumeka told me that it had affected her ideas of herself and the world. And indeed her life changed. She became more peaceful and contented and opened up to new spiritual possibilities.

The most devastating initiation is the fourth one, known as the crucifixion. Jesus took his on the cross. It involves the offering of yourself at an emotional level and tests your deepest fears in order to lift some of the fear in the collective consciousness. It often involves rejection and loss on a personal and emotional level. However, on a spiritual level it is the gateway to something higher.

A friend of mine took this initiation by suffering the loss of both her sons and grandchildren, who suddenly moved away to the other side of the world. They had been her whole life. She had to adjust, and became a healer, devoting her life to helping others. A few years later she undertook another initiation through the illness of her sister.

My crucifixion lasted for nearly twenty years. Again it was to do with loss of everything I had known. Now I understand that the emotional trauma was an amazing opportunity for spiritual growth, which was orchestrated by my guides and angels. It presented me with the circumstances for my fourth initiation. At the same time it presented most of my family with an opportunity to undertake their second or third initiations.

What seemed like many shattered lives was, from a higher perspective, a huge spiritual opportunity. I bless everyone concerned. It also demonstrates graphically to me that no one can ever judge another. I had to let go of everything in order to let the angels into my life.

Some people have a very difficult time taking their fifth initiation, which is the preparation for the ascension path. This is where you have access to your Monad or I AM presence and sign on for cosmic service. This initiation was easy for me, as I had done it so many times in other lives. In response to feeling that this was the right time, I met two friends and we took each other through a meditation into the first stages of ascension. Interestingly one of them achieved it first, and then he helped us through.

The sixth initiation is ascension and for many this is relatively easy after the preparation they have undergone, though if you have read Elizabeth Haitch's fascinating book called *Initiation*, this is the one she failed. The consequences of failure are quite dire. In her case she had to start again at the beginning and learn the lessons of life. It was rather like a university graduate having to go back to kindergarten again. I know someone else who failed this initiation and had to reincarnate with great wisdom but no power to express it.

There is a seventh initiation. It is taken out of body after death and takes place during discussions about your next step. In order to pass it you must be willing to do that which is for the highest good.

EXERCISE: *Review your Tests and Challenges*

Take time to examine the tests and challenges you have undergone to become the person you are. Have any of them changed you? Looking back on your life can you see yourself and other people differently knowing that you had to experience what you went through in order to get you where you are now?

2032 and Beyond

CHAPTER 31

Technology by 2032

PEOPLE OFTEN ASK ME if there will be mobile phones and televisions in 2032. What will have happened to the Internet? Will there be cars?

By 2032 most people will have anchored their twelve chakras and will have opened psychically and spiritually to some of their genetically encoded gifts. People will then generally communicate telepathically or at least be so attuned to each other that telephones will not be necessary. However, there will still be a few people who will communicate by phone. More importantly they will still be using some of the same frequency bands that are so harmful to the bees, dolphins and whales. But it will no longer be as widespread and all-enveloping. There will also be much more awareness of the damage that can be inflicted by certain wavelengths and people will avoid them.

Will people have televisions then? Quite possibly in their attics or forgotten in some shed. Technology will have moved on and no one will want a TV. It is rather like asking someone now if they still have a gramophone.

The Internet will still be available though it will be much more sophisticated than what we have now and based on spiritual technology, similar to that in Golden Atlantis. The wave bands will be a much higher frequency and will only carry positive or inspiring material and information. Since most of the population will be fifth-dimensional they will not be interested in the sort of traffic that is currently transmitted.

~ Spiritual Technology ~

On the one hand life will be quite simple and natural. On the other there will be awesome spiritual technology available which is nothing like we know now. Every single thing will be on a much higher frequency and we cannot imagine it.

The angels long ago promised that they would make themselves visible to humanity. They did so by impressing open-minded scientists to create digital cameras at a frequency the spiritual realms could work with. The angels were then able to bring their vibration down so that their light bodies could be caught on film. The result of this is the occurrence of Orbs which have caused such a worldwide sensation as people become aware that they are angels. In the same way more scientists will be consciously or unconsciously receiving downloads from spirit and developing them for the benefit of humanity.

Subatomic physics is telling us that the thoughts of the experimenter affect the result of the experiment, but this is only the tip of the iceberg. Soon physicists will recognize that focused thought, especially if a number of people trained in mind control work together, can manifest physical objects. As fifth-dimensional humans develop their higher minds and concentrate on creation for the highest good of all, there will be an exponential shift in our understanding and use of our powers. When we open up to our full psychic potential again, we will be able to create extraordinary and beneficial things.

Crystal technology will have developed well beyond the use of silicone chips in computers, so crystals will be programmed once more to help humanity.

Laser lights will be used to knit bones. They will even be able to heal spinal fractures using lasers with the power of thought and intention. The new medicine will be about balancing people's chakras with sound and light, though herbs and natural products will help everyone maintain the maximum flow of energy to their bodies. Healers will use their minds to raise the person needing attention into the light of Divine Perfection, so that perfect health is maintained.

Everything will be biodegradable. We will see vehicles made from plant material and they will be powered by plant oils or water. Plant products will be refined into pliable, durable and ecological materials, which will replace products made from oil and most metals.

~ *Space Craft* ~

With the new technology and materials available, humans will once more explore space. More advanced exploration will only be allowed when international peace and co-operation is established. Then the projects will be successful for the intention will be different from that in current times. The energy of the challenger will transform into something humble and filled with awe. When humans are moved by a desire to explore God's creation and connect lovingly with other star systems, then the spiritual realms will work in harmony with science.

~ Lighting and Heating ~

This will be provided by sunlight or other natural energy, captured into compact batteries. People will also be able to light up crystals as they did in Golden Atlantis.

There is a divine paradox in the technology of the New Golden Age. As technological advances mean we can do amazing things again more people will want to reconnect to the love of the Earth. Gardening, walking, mountain climbing, cycling and outdoor sports of all kinds will become more popular than ever before.

~ Clothes ~

New materials will have been discovered which are light, breathable and provide the perfect temperature for people. Throughout the world a consensus will choose to don simple all in one suits, a little like cat suits that are suitable for summer and winter, inside and out and incredibly easy to wear.

But, there will be many, especially women who have been repressed for years, who will choose to express their femininity by wearing pretty dresses in dazzling materials. Men too will become freer in the clothes they wear. However fashion will not be important.

There will be no ego, no rivalry, so everyone will be happy to express their true essence as they wish to.

EXERCISE: *Visualization for Creativity*

Master Hilarion, Master of the fifth ray, which is orange, helps to bring in new science and technology. He whispers to inventors, inspiring them to create things that will help humanity. Millions of angels work with him.

1. Sit quietly where you are undisturbed.
2. Hold a vision of a world where we are assisted by awesome,

inspiring, spiritual technology, for example a spiritual Internet, free energy that powers us to fly. Let your imagination flow.

3. Imagine you are holding an orange ball of light between your hands. It is getting bigger and brighter with every new thought you have.

4. Visualize angels taking some of the orange energy you have just created.

5. They are using your energy to whisper to scientists, inventors, physicists, surgeons, vets, doctors and others, opening them up to new possibilities.

6. Accept their thanks for helping to co-create a beautiful future.

7. Open your eyes.

CHAPTER 32

Leadership

IT IS SAID that cultures get the leaders they deserve. The Law of Attraction tells us we attract reflections of our inner being. Third-dimensional humanity votes for low quality leaders.

For centuries we have had masculine-dominated politics. On their negative side they display qualities like: controlling, logical without heart, authoritarian, divisive and short term. On the positive site they are logical, considered, numerate and they take action so that change is possible and conditions move forward.

In 2008/2009 a new energy came into the planet, exactly as forecast in the Mayan Calendar. It drew underhand behaviour, cheating and abuse to the surface to be exposed and cleaned up.

Also in 2008 the Silver Ray of the Divine Feminine entered the planet for the first time since Atlantis. It has merged with all the ascended masters and angels and is now starting to touch humanity. The Silver Ray is bringing forward the feminine qualities traditionally regarded as the preserve of women: co-operation, support, working for the good of the whole rather than the individual, covering for those who need help, speaking your truth, listening rather than forcing your views on others. Already these qualities are subtly influencing everyone.

Because the Silver Ray has a very high frequency, those in positions of power who cannot cope with its energy, are quitting their posts. The workers are feeling it and starting to expect their leaders to demonstrate higher moral fibre and honesty. This ray is dissolving the old masculine paradigm and touching the consciousness of the people with the new.

The power truly lies with the population. In the third-dimensional world we have given it away to politicians and big business. To enter the new, we must claim it back.

If enough people can align themselves to the higher truth, the changes will take place like a gentle breeze.

~ *The Transition Years* ~

The light coming in during 2012 will raise people's self-worth and confidence. As the consciousness rises, individuals will start to love themselves and recognize their divine essence. They will integrate their inner personalities and therefore act with integrity and honesty. Then they will feel happy about themselves, so they will be open and ready to empower others.

When you love and trust yourself, you do not seek authority or guidance from someone outside yourself. You rely on your inner wisdom.

During the twenty-year transition between 2012 and 2032 there will be a huge shift in the way cultures perceive themselves and the rest of the world. In the challenging times of cleansing and weather disruption, people from different countries will work together and support each other and this will leave a lasting feeling of goodwill towards others and an understanding that we are all the same, we are all one. They will no longer look with eyes of fear, suspicion and judgement but increasingly with eyes of love, trust and acceptance.

People will look back with amazement at adversarial politics, bullying tactics and dictatorships. The idea of owning or enslaving another soul will be an anathema. Yet in some traditional patriarchal societies or those with very entrenched views, there may be resistance, which comes from fear and control and will hold everyone back. When you resist you focus on what you do not want. The way forward is to embrace what is for the highest good. Every individual who is ready for equality, fairness, justice and empowerment of all can assist by visualizing the new and calling in the Silver Flame.

> *My grandmother, who was a very special, warm-hearted lady, had a little plaque in her guest room, which read:*
>
> *Hail guest, we ask not what thou art*
> *If friend we greet thee hand and heart*
> *If stranger, such no longer be*
> *If foe, our love will conquer thee.*

To me this encapsulates the way families and countries will behave towards each other as the transition period progresses.

Soon honourable people will emerge to inspire the world through the transition. During this period honesty, integrity, openness and the ability to empower others will be qualities that are increasingly respected.

~ 2032 ~

By 2032 so many people will see or sense the energy fields of others, that there will be nothing hidden. All will be transparent.

The old souls being born in the period up to 2032 are being prepared to be strong, wise, caring, co-operative and enlightened so that they can work honourably for the highest good of all.

Community life will be so different from our current political paradigm that it will be almost unimaginable to us in our present state of consciousness. I originally called this chapter Leadership and Government but Kumeka asked me to take out the word Government as it implies control and there will be no such thing by 2032. There will be no pyramid of power, no leaders. Instead everyone will work together for the highest good, so decisions will evolve automatically.

By 2032 people will mostly be vibrating in the fifth dimension where they recognize that there is no them and us, just us. So on all the continents, communities will be welcoming and supportive of each other. As a world we will share technology and new ideas. Everywhere people will work for the highest good as they co-create a new world.

Within communities, countries and the world people will become co-creators with each other and the divine. All choices will arise for the highest good.

EXERCISE: *Practice Co-operation*

In order to align ourselves with the new higher energies, we have to practise acting with those qualities. So practice co-operation. Co-create something with others, however small. Make enlightened decisions. Every time you do this it brings the possibility nearer for everyone.

CHAPTER 33

Living in the
Fifth Dimension

AFTER 2012 those who are ready will be able to carry more light. This will be needed to help the masses, for Mother Earth will continue to purify the planet. Many will be frightened by the changes and light-workers are being prepared who will act as beacons and teachers. For those who are ready there is a great deal to be done and many opportunities for accelerated spiritual growth available.

At the fifth dimension your chakras will be glowing with light.

How to Live in the Fifth Dimension

~ Treat others, as you would like them to treat you ~

The first practice of living in the fifth dimension is to do as you would be done by. Constantly think how others feel and would like to be treated. So if you see someone holding back because they are shy, gently draw them into the circle. If you see a creature lost or in pain, help it. It is inappropriate to be a rescuer, one who helps needy people because it covers up their own neediness by making them feel good. That is an aspect of the third dimension. At the fifth dimension you are responding to the needs of others without a personal hidden agenda. As a result the universe rewards you tenfold.

~ Do things that are for your highest good ~

If something is not for your highest good it is not for the highest good of others either. The converse is also true. If it is not for someone else's benefit it is not going to serve your soul either. So always act with this in mind.

~ Keep your heart open ~

Act with loving kindness at all times. If someone acts unkindly towards you or hurts you, bless them with love.

~ Prioritize your life so that you have more leisure ~

You cannot be busy, busy, busy and maintain your vibration in the fifth dimension, so take time out to relax, meditate and enjoy life.

~ Treat things lightly so that you enjoy fun and laughter ~

Watch your attitude! Take things lightly. Choose laughter as a response. You will feel happier and so will people around you.

~ Surround yourself with high frequency people ~

Take a decision about those who raise your frequency and those who bring it down. If this means walking alone or having fewer friends for a time until you attract in the new, that is a choice you have to make.

~ Keep your home in the vibration of the fifth dimension ~

Make your home as harmonious as possible. This does not mean that you become a doormat to keep people happy. It implies strength, mastery and the ability to raise the frequency of those in your household. At the same time your home needs to be clean, happy and a safe refuge. Flowers, beautiful music and colours help.

~ Emanate a vibration, which attracts work that satisfies you ~

In this higher dimension you take mastery of your life and your energy fields. So you align your frequency to that of work, which suits your temperament and deeply satisfies your soul. You may find the information and exercises in the chapter on Abundance and Manifestation helpful.

~ Live with abundance consciousness ~

Watch your thoughts and words. Make sure all your thoughts and statements align with the highest possibilities. Do not drag your vision down with doubts, fears and poverty consciousness. Be generous.

~ Live as a Master ~

Always act with integrity, honour and responsibility.

~ Connect constantly with your Earth Star Chakra through your connection with the Earth ~

Your Earth Star Chakra, 12 inches or 30 cms below your feet, is your spiritual foundation. Unless it is awake, open and active you cannot ascend. You are like a tall building, the more secure your foundations are, the higher you can grow. The seeds of your potential are nurtured here by Archangel Sandalphon, so if you want to fulfil your highest destiny, make sure you connect with this chakra. Any activity where you are in contact with the earth is good. Walking, climbing, playing in a meadow as you picnic, standing barefoot in the grass, growing flowers and vegetables all help you to be connected to your Earth Star Chakra. It is better to walk on ground rather than tarmac if you possibly can.

~ Have a symbiotic relationship with plants, trees and all of nature ~

When you hug a tree, you can open up to the knowledge and wisdom it holds and at the same time its roots help your roots to move down deeply into your Earth Star Chakra. Being in nature keeps you in balance and harmony and really helps you to maintain a fifth-dimensional frequency.

~ Walk with the elementals, angels and spirit world ~

When you are a fifth-dimensional being you are automatically aware of the spiritual dimensions around you. Take that extra step and walk hand-in-hand with angels in your daily life. Be aware of the work the elementals are doing all around you and also be open to those spirit visitors who have passed through the veil but still connect to Earth.

~ Listen to the divine promptings ~

Watch for signs and always listen to the promptings of the divine. This is part of fifth-dimensional attunement.

~ Eat appropriate food ~

Eat lightly the foods that have a high vibration matching your own. Fifth-dimensional foods are organically grown. Eat as many green vegetables as possible, fruits, nuts and as nutritionally balanced a diet as possible. Bless your food before you consume it. Remember that you may need some heavier food to keep you grounded and honour this. You cannot be in the fifth dimension if you are floating about like a space cadet. There must be balance.

~ Have a spiritual attitude to all things ~

Look for the highest perspective in all situations and people. Bless that which is of lower frequency to bring it up to a higher level.

~ Radiate wisdom from your solar plexus ~

Your solar plexus is a huge psychic pump, which at the third dimension seeks danger so that you can avoid it. At a higher level, its antennae reach to the energy fields of Archangel Uriel, the archangel in charge of the development of the solar plexus, and trust him to keep you safe. You can then bring forward your own wisdom and soothe the fears of others. It is really helpful to visualize this while out in nature.

~ Work with your twelve chakras ~

Frequently attune and energize your twelve chakras. You can do this at any time, when sitting quietly, walking in nature, waiting for something, doing housework or as a passenger in a car or any form of transport. This is not a meditation and is done with your eyes open. All you have to do is mentally focus on each chakra for a moment and ask the appropriate angels to align them to bring Source energy through you.

Mentally ask for each one in turn.

LIVING IN THE FIFTH DIMENSION

- **Archangel Sandalphon**, please open and align my Earth Star Chakra.
- **Archangel Gabriel,** please open and align my base chakra.
- **Archangel Gabriel,** please open and align my sacral chakra.
- **Archangel Gabriel,** please open and align my navel chakra.
- **Archangel Uriel,** please open and align my solar plexus chakra.
- **Archangel Chamuel,** please open and align my heart chakra.
- **Archangel Michael,** please open and align my throat chakra.
- **Archangel Raphael,** please open and align my third eye chakra.
- **Archangel Jophiel,** please open and align my crown chakra.
- **Archangel Christiel**, please open and align my causal chakra.
- **Archangels Zadkiel and Mariel**, please open and align my soul star chakra.
- **Archangel Metatron**, please open and align my Stellar Gateway chakra.

A very powerful alternative is to look at Orbs of the Archangels of each chakra. This will set you ablaze with light. They can be found in the book *Ascension Through Orbs* that I co-wrote with Kathy Crosswell.

~ Connect with Archangel Metatron ~

Daily invoke Archangel Metatron in his gold and orange light and ask him to help you on your ascension path.

~ Remember you are Part of Oneness ~

Look at the great open sky, the stars, the moon, the sun and the entire cosmos and remember that it is one great organism with you being part of it and connected to every living thing in it.

~ Invoke Fifth-Dimensional Bubbles ~

Archangel Sandalphon who is in charge of the Earth Star Chakra will place a fifth-dimensional bubble round you if you ask him to.

You can also ask him to place them around other people with their consent or if you have tuned into their higher self to receive permission. For a few days I asked Archangel Sandalphon to place a fifth-dimensional bubble round a friend because I thought it would help him. I noticed that he became more and more confused and depressed and wondered if it was the bubble. I checked with Kumeka, who told me to stop, as he was not ready for it and it was affecting him! I felt awful!

I was telling another friend about the bubbles and he lit up like a beacon. He asked me to place one round him when I do my daily attunements. A couple of days later he phoned to say he had felt it each time I had sent it. His mind was totally clear now and he literally felt it lifting him into a higher space and keeping him there.

If you feel you are ready and wish to call one in do this visualization.

EXERCISE: *Visualization to Raise your Frequency*

1. Find a place where you can be quiet and undisturbed.
2. Breathe comfortably until you feel relaxed.
3. Invoke Archangel Sandalphon and sense his presence beside you.
4. Mentally ask him to place you in a fifth-dimensional bubble.
5. Sense, see or feel this over you.
6. Relax into it and accept that it is raising your frequency.
7. If you wish to ask Archangel Sandalphon to place bubbles of the fifth dimension round other people, do so now. Make sure you have their consent or very clear guidance to do so.
8. Thank Archangel Sandalphon.
9. Open your eyes and consciously think and act in a higher way.

EXERCISE: *Maintaining your Solar Plexus Chakra in the Fifth Dimension*

1. Find a place where you can be quiet and undisturbed.
2. Breathe comfortably until you feel relaxed.
3. Imagine a deep gold sun shining into your solar plexus.
4. On your inbreath take in the warmth and wisdom of this golden light.
5. On each outbreath release any greenish yellow fear from your solar plexus.
6. Visualize a fifth-dimensional cord moving from your solar plexus and connecting into Archangel Uriel's energy field. Know that he will protect you.
7. Thank Archangel Uriel and open your eyes.

CHAPTER 34

The New Golden Cities

SOON AFTER 2032 new, fifth-dimensional golden cities will arise all over the planet. Most, but not all of them, will be constructed in mountains where the land has been purified and the air is clear. I'm told they are almost impossible to envisage according to our current consciousness. They are called golden cities because their energy will be golden.

Because the population will be much lower there will be no land pressure, so the cities will be spacious, green and gracious and much smaller than our current concept of a city.

Houses will be single or double story only as it will be realized that we lose our connection with the Earth in high-rise apartment blocks. Each city will be based round a natural spring for throughout the world pure running water will be used to raise the energy of places. Nowhere will the water be chemically polluted but it will be kept pure and clear with crystals and magnets.

There will be no planning departments or government regulations or ego, so the roads and buildings will evolve for the highest good of the residents who are attuned to the vision of harmony. According to our current consciousness this would result in chaos and anarchy. However, in a fifth-dimensional world, the highest choices flow naturally from the hearts and visions of those involved.

Trees and natural geological formations will be highly respected and buildings will be created round them. The homes will be communally built by willing, generous-hearted people all happy to help their friends, family or strangers alike. They will understand that we are all one.

For the past few thousand years towns and buildings have been constructed according to the masculine energy, square, rigid, linear, straight, individually regimented and angular. The residents of the future will look with horror at our way of living. What we call personal space they will consider lonely and isolated.

By the time the new golden cities flower the influence of the divine feminine will be felt everywhere. It is flowing, fun, creative, communal, rounded and beautiful. Furthermore spiritual technology will have developed, allowing the production of curves and flowing structures.

So houses will be built of strong biodegradable plant material, which can be extruded into wonderful curved shapes and colours, with windows that are round or oblong. And the homes will nestle into the contours of the land. They will be built in clusters with communal, shared facilities, which will be considered friendly and less wasteful.

Fun elements will be built into the homes, like a slide or a zip wire down the hillside from the gardens to the school, which will then magnetically pull you up again when you are ready to return.

Individual ownership, which is based on a belief in lack, will cease to be. Within the city will be lakes and streams where communally owned boats or canoes will be moored in designated places for the use of everyone. Water sports will be popular, especially where it is warm, partly because the purifying qualities of that element will be recognized and partly because they are fun.

Sports facilities will be widely available everywhere for anyone to use freely. The children being born in the next twenty years will continue to be high-frequency, high-energy souls who need to express themselves physically. In the fifth-dimensional consciousness, there is no place for dishonesty or stealing, so sports equipment will be left in the halls or open spaces for all to share. People will be less inhibited or shy, so they will naturally congregate and draw everyone in to participate in team games or any social activities.

Vehicles will be produced from biodegradable material, run on ecological fuel, and shared communally. In the higher consciousness there is an understanding that your needs will always be met. Accordingly a vehicle will always be in the perfect place at the perfect time for whoever needs it. There will also be transports, some operated by volunteers and others remotely, which run from place to place according to need.

To travel greater distances small vehicles will hook up to an engine, which will take them all at unbelievable speeds on an air cushion, rather like a hovercraft, to a designated place. There they will unhook and continue to their final destination.

By this time a number of people will be able to levitate and transport themselves short distances. Eventually ecologically powered planes, shaped like rockets, will transport people across the world at speeds beyond our comprehension, but this will not be until 2050 or thereabouts.

Health and safety will be the subject of derision to be replaced with common sense and individual responsibility. Because everyone will be doing things for the highest good, they will all be naturally sensible without being ridiculously overprotective.

Music will be very popular, especially as the power and importance of sound and harmony is truly comprehended. Everyone will have an opportunity to learn to play a musical instrument. As with sports equipment, vehicles and boats, musical instruments will be freely available and shared and treated with care. If someone needs to attune to a particular one, this will be understood and respected, so they will use that guitar or flute or whatever as long as they need it. People will gather in groups to play music together or to listen to it. All music will be harmonious because it will reflect the spirit of the player. Only those out of synch internally play or listen to discordant music.

As with music, creative expression of all kinds will be encouraged, whether you are a child or adult. People will have the opportunity to draw, paint, design, create, sing or develop themselves in the right way for their soul.

~ Work ~

The fifth-dimensional world is one without ego, power struggle, personal drive or ambition, just a desire to express yourself creatively, serve others, connect with the Earth and attune to the spiritual dimensions. This may seem boring to those who are caught up in the dramas of personality struggle and emotional need. In fact it will offer a wondrous sense of joy, contentment and peace.

It will be considered important to do what fulfils you and makes you happy, and the people will spend their time being creative and happily productive. There will be no money or banks, just energy exchange.

Without the inner drive to build a business or succeed at a job, people will co-operate happily to produce what is necessary for their needs. Anything extra will be pooled and freely exchanged.

~ Food ~

Most people will be vegetarian, though a number will eat fish. As people raise their frequency they have less need of heavy foods, so the demand will be for simple, healthy things to consume.

~ Waste ~

There will be no plastics, no supermarkets and no demand to wrap goods. Anything that needs to be protected will be wrapped in ecological reusable materials, not invented yet.

New cooling methods will obviate the need for refrigeration and ways of producing fresh produce throughout the year will mean freezing as a storage method becomes obsolete in all but a few places. So these items will not need to be disposed of.

It will be some time before the de-materialization techniques that were used in Atlantis on rubbish are once more in operation.

Where people have self-worth they value their surroundings. So in these golden cities litter or illegal dumping will be unheard of. All spaces will be clean and beautiful.

~ Flowers and Trees ~

Trees will be highly respected and people will communicate with the elementals that live in them. Many will be planted, both for the ecology of the planet and individual gracious specimens to admire.

Flowers will cascade everywhere for the new golden cities will be alive with glorious sculptures, artwork, fountains and flowers.

Because of changed climatic and geographical conditions some may be underground, on water or very different from that which we can imagine. But the high-frequency light of the inhabitants will mean that they can live happily, harmoniously and ecologically in new ways.

EXERCISE: *Make your Home or Office Golden*

You can make the energy of your home or work place more golden by beautifying it, filling it with harmonious objects, music, flowers and most importantly golden thoughts. Start now doing what you can.

CHAPTER 35

Kumeka,
Lord of Light

WHEN SOURCE created the divine sparks, he first sent out twelve sparks. If you imagine someone having twelve children, these Monads were of his energy like his sons and daughters. After that the divine sparks were created through the sons and daughters. They were his energy as if they were his grandchildren. One of the original divine sparks was the Monad of Jesus, who incarnated on our planet to try to change the world. This is why he is known as the Son of God. He is now on the Board of the Lords of Karma in charge of the eighth ray and is also the Bringer of Cosmic Love.

Kumeka is another one of the original twelve and he was assigned to another universe, where he ascended becoming a Lord of Light. He approached this universe during Atlantis and worked with the Intergalactic Council as an adviser on the setting up of Atlantis when he helped to oversee the Golden Age.

Like many great beings, he withdrew from this universe when the energy frequency dropped at the end of Atlantis and the islands were submerged. Now at the end of the 260,000-year Atlantean period, he has returned to help with the very end of the old and the beginning of the new. Earth has earned the right to his guidance once more. He is the Master of the eighth ray, working closely with Jesus who is the Lord of Karma for this ray.

Kumeka has never incarnated and does not really know what it is like to have a human body. Anyone who has inhabited a physical body on Earth is conducted on their travels by angels. This includes all the Ascended Masters, such as Quan Yin or Lord Kuthumi. As they go about their business there is always an angel with them so if you photograph them as an Orb, you will see the circle of angel energy round them. However, as Kumeka has never had an Earth experience he travels independently. His blue Orb is unique in that it has a mound in the middle. This is because he is constantly pushing out his energy to touch people, while the angels embrace humans into their Orbs.

I feel very privileged that Kumeka is my main guide. He comes from the same universe as I do, but not from the same planet. I have written elsewhere about my first meeting with him, one New Year's Eve, which I spent with my later co-author of *Discover Atlantis*, Shaaron Hutton. As we were meditating together a mighty energy entered the room and introduced himself as Kumeka, saying he wanted to work through us. That evening was one of the most exciting of my life. His etheric retreat and entry portal is in Caracas, Venezuela. He told me he had first seen my light while I was living near there and had been waiting for me to be ready.

His colour is blue and he has twice impressed on me to buy topaz rings. The first was quite small and he later told me that he and my guardian angel had pushed me into the shop. When I declined to buy it, the topaz light flashed in my third eye all night, until I got the message and went back and bought it. When I earned promotion to a bigger, more connecting topaz, I got the message immediately! I do not really need to wear the ring now to connect with him, but he still sometimes sends me to fetch it when he wants to give me detailed information.

When he first connected to Shaaron and myself, we were his only channels. He asked me to tell people about him in my books and also to ask Andrew Brel to write music for him. Now Kumeka can divide into an infinite number of parts and channels his energy and information through hundreds of thousands of people. In fact, he can divide himself up as many times as is needed.

~ Spearheading the Move to Enlightenment ~

Kumeka is helping to enlighten Earth as well as the four ascension planets in this universe. He is performing the same service to other planets in other universes.

In his work for Earth he is specifically working with the following great beings.

ARCHANGEL METATRON is in charge of the development of the Stellar Gateway and is overseeing the current movement to ascension.

THE UNICORNS, the purest of the pure, are helping to dissolve the veils of illusion over the third eye.

WYWYVSIL is a very fast-frequency angel known as a Power. He is a Lord of Karma and the Angel of Birth. He has set up a number of schools in the inner planes to teach healing, enlightenment and transformation to those who have sufficient light. If you are ready you can ask that your spirit attend these schools during your sleep. In Atlantis, he created with others a pool of energy for healing, transformation and enlightenment, and he is sending light from this directly to Earth, which you can access. He is working with the seraphim to help creation.

AZARIEL is a great archangel who is working with the unicorns to bring forward enlightenment and ascension. She specially clears the energies round the third eye and crown.

SERAPHINA is the seraphim who is helping Metatron to develop your Stellar Gateway. She then helps to fine tune the energy to it from Source, so that you can ascend.

To a lesser extent Kumeka also works with Archangels Gabriel, Michael, Uriel and Raphael.

You can find much more information about these mighty beings in the book *Ascension Through Orbs*.

Kumeka is master of the eighth ray of deep cleansing. He takes the purification and transmutation offered by Archangels Gabriel and Zadkiel to a much deeper level.

Like all the great masters and archangels he is totally merged with the Silver Ray.

~ Healing ~

When you vibrate in the fifth-dimensional frequency, you can ask him to awaken all the cells in your body , which will totally heal you. You have released the 4th veil of illusion by this time. As time moves on more people can access this help.

*Kathy Crosswell and I were both talking to him when he told
us this so we asked him to do it for us. We both felt fizzing
inside and as if light was sparkling out of us.*

I expected instant healing for a problem with my hands but he told me I
had to take responsibility for the food I ate and take suitable exercise. I
also had to talk to him and the elementals more and completely balance
my life.

Kumeka indicated that we are also responsible for the fat on our
bodies. He said we need to eat green food to clear the waste between
our cells, then the elementals, especially the earth elementals, would
work inside our bodies to help us through the medium of the green
food. Next morning I had lettuce for breakfast but that resolution did
not last long!

MEDITATION: *Linking with Kumeka*

If you think about Kumeka he will come to you.

1. Find a place where you can be quiet and relaxed.
2. Close your eyes and visualize a blue light, the colour of blue topaz.
3. Ask Kumeka, Lord of Light and Master of the eighth ray, to come
   to you.
4. You may sense a presence on your left hand side. If you cannot see
   or sense him, trust that he is there.
5. Ask him to help you with deep cleansing and enlightenment.
6. His response may come to you as a thought or a flash of inspiration. He will always ask you to do something to help yourself. If this
   does not happen, know that he will be subtly guiding you to do
   things that will help you.
7. Sit quietly for a few minutes in Kumeka's light.
8. Thank him for coming.
9. Open your eyes.

CHAPTER 36

Archangel Metatron

WE REFER TO HIM as Archangel Metatron but in reality he is a great Universal Angel whose energy reaches out into the cosmos and influences many planes of existence. Because of this, he and his twin flame Sandalphon, who is also a Universal Angel are known as the tall angels.

Metatron is known as 'The Prince of the Countenance' because he is the only angel allowed to look into the light of Source. He comes from Orion, the planet of wisdom.

Our universe is like an orchestra. Source is the composer. Metatron is the conductor and he is concentrating on Earth because we are the only planet in the universe that is off key. Metatron is now rapidly re-tuning us so that the whole can play in harmony again.

~ Why was Earth allowed to get so Out of Synch? ~

This was the outcome of the divine gift of free will. It was originally envisaged that humans would use it to co-create wondrous things, but in the event, we used it to go flat, delving deeper into the material and sexual and controlling our fellow beings.

This resulted in karma or bad debts, which have to be repaid. Once free will has been accepted humans have to take responsibility for the consequences. They must reincarnate and balance it. It is easier to do it on this planet because of the feedback mechanism of the body, which is built from soul choices and shaped by our daily thoughts, emotions, as well as by how we treat it with exercise, food and drink intake. Our body tells us what is going on and whether we as individuals are in harmony or not.

Because Earth is rising in frequency once more Source and Metatron together magnanimously offered to allow all those who have ever incarnated an opportunity to balance their karma before the changes take place. Not everyone is succeeding. This is just one of the reasons for gross overpopulation.

Metatron's colour is orange, a mix of gold and red. The gold is the vibration of deepest wisdom, merged with the Christ consciousness of love and the angelic frequency. The red is the raw masculine creative power of Source, which gives him the energy to take action. The orange radiates joy and happiness.

Years ago, before I knew I was so very connected to Metatron I chose the most beautiful soft golden orange colour scheme for my bedroom, bathroom and adjoining office. He now tells me that he inspired me to choose it to help attune to him while I slept or worked and to bring forward his wisdom. It is also the most wonderful restful colour.

Metatron vibrates on the number twelve, the number of discipleship. This insists that those who attune to him become spiritually disciplined.

He is in charge of the development of the Stellar Gateway chakra, the ultimate spiritual centre of the body, which receives Source energy. Here we merge with our original divine sparks or Monads, also known as the I AM Presence. Metatron co-operates here with Seraphina and the Universal Angel Butyalil to build the final ladder to Source.

~ *Connection with Egypt* ~

Metatron has an entry point on every star, planet or constellation in this universe. On Earth it is Luxor. This is because it is the home of the Sphinx and the great pyramid of Giza, with which he has powerful connections. Because of his vast knowledge and wisdom at the end of Atlantis and because he brought through Sacred Geometry from Source he oversaw the building of the pyramids of Egypt, and energized them with cosmic light. They are vast cosmic computers that link us to the cosmos.

He is known as the Heavenly Scribe for he is in charge of the heavenly archives, supervising the karmic records, which are held within the Sphinx at a higher dimension. He also oversees the recording angels and passes the daily orders of Source to all the Archangels in such a way that they can be transmitted to the entire realm of angels.

The Universal Angel Metatron works with Thoth, the great priest avatar of Atlantis. He is known as the Egyptian Scribe, for he keeps the akashic records of the Egyptian races and all the Arab countries.

Metatron also oversees Enoch, the wise sage, and Serapis Bey. The latter, who originated from Venus, is the Master of the fourth ray of Harmony and Balance, He was a priest avatar in Atlantis and Keeper of the White Flame. Serapis Bey is known as The Egyptian because at the fall of Atlantis he worked with Archangel Metatron and his angels to influence the building of the pyramids, where his teachings are hidden at a fourth-dimensional level.

~ Metatron's Cube ~

This is a sacred geometrical plan showing the cosmic connections within this universe. Based on every single thing being linked and interlinked, it demonstrates a triangular formation. The basic unit is a triangle, which is very strong and stable. When twelve places, planets or people are linked, they create four triangles. Twelve is Metatron's number. When twelve segments of twelve join together there are 144 connections. This becomes a whole and a new construct is formed.

My guide Kumeka told me that Metatron would give me the information for this chapter. I woke in the night and wrote down some notes that came to me. As I was doing this I glanced at the clock and saw it was 0.4.40. As 44 is the number of Golden Atlantis it keyed me to ask mentally what was his connection with that era.

Metatron told me that he conceived the idea for the fifth experiment of Atlantis, which produced the Golden Age. The previous four had failed dismally as humans fell into disharmony and desired power. This time he decided that those who populated the remaining Atlantean islands would start with nothing, which would force them to co-operate and co-create a community together. Metatron oversaw this controlled experiment with Kumeka. They advised the Intergalactic Council who looked after the details. I write fully in *Discover Atlantis* how the extraordinary experiment of Golden Atlantis was set up and evolved into the only time of Heaven on Earth there has ever been on this planet.

When I finished writing I dropped my note pad onto the floor by my bed and saw an Orb photo of Metatron lying there! By it was one of the Universal Angel, Purlimiek, who is in charge of the nature kingdom. They certainly were not there when I went to bed! I believe that the two

Orb cards appeared to remind me that the final experiment was so successful primarily because the citizens worked so closely with nature.

~ Metatron's Orange and Gold Cloak ~

I mention in the introduction that I was given Metatron's orange and gold cloak while I was writing this book. He told me that once you have received it, you do not have to put it on for it is always there. Nor can it be taken away. You become the High Priest or Priestess and to attain this honour you must have been one in a past life. The High Priests and Priestesses from the entire past of the planet are returning now.

Metatron is a mighty being. He has so much energy and power that it can be felt everywhere in the universe in a single instant. When you wear the cloak you too can be felt everywhere. I was told it must always be used with compassion. When you stand tall, connected to Heaven and Earth, with your heart open so that people feel they can approach you, then the cloak automatically does its work.

EXERCISE: *Write to Archangel Metatron*

Make sure you have paper and pencil or pen. The more focus and passion you put into this, the clearer the response.

1. Light a candle if you can and dedicate it to connecting with Archangel Metatron.
2. Sit quietly and think about Archangel Metatron for a few minutes.
3. Breathe a beautiful gold colour around you, then red, then bright orange. Let the colours swirl together until you are bathed in glorious orange.
4. Write, 'Dear Archangel Metatron,' on your piece of paper.
5. Thank him for what he has done. Ask him any questions. Ask him to connect with you more often. Tell him what you want to.
6. Then sign off with love and your name.

You may be happy just to write the letter and keep it in a safe place or burn it, knowing that you will receive a response in due course in some way from the archangel. Alternatively you may wish to take another piece of paper and prepare to receive a response. In this case, write Dear and your own name.

Then put the tip of the pen on the paper and let a response flow through you. Do not censor it. Just write whatever comes to you and you may be surprised at the guidance or information you receive. If it is full of light and is helpful and loving, trust it is from Archangel Metatron. If it is not, then you are not tuned into an angel, so close down and destroy the letter.

After I wrote this I asked Metatron if he was happy for everyone to write to him. His reply was one word, 'Yes!'

CHAPTER 37

Religion and Spirituality

RELIGION HAS BEEN a divisive force for thousands of years. Over the aeons Source has sent archangels and great masters who have taught of love, forgiveness and Oneness to enlighten the world.

Their teachings have subsequently been distorted by the egos of their followers, who desired to control by spreading fear and limitation. Yet religions have done much good. They have offered comfort and hope to the masses at a time when their consciousness was closed to true spirituality.

By 2032 as a world we will have moved beyond the confines of dogma. Spirituality will be a cohesive and joyous light between all nations.

Spirituality talks only of love and togetherness. It heals, empowers and inspires. It seeks the divine spark within the hearts of all and fans it into a flame. That will be the guiding force of the new Golden Age.

Archangels Mariel and Lavender, who are in charge of the Soul Star chakra, are helping to influence everyone on the planet at a soul level to aspire to spirituality rather than religion.

~ Acceptance ~

At a deep inner level everyone wants to be kind, loving, happy, generous, honest, sunny, confident, friendly and trusting. If you judge or criticize another with so much as a thought, they will pick it up and react. Up will come the drawbridge to their heart and out will come the shield to defend or the arrows to attack. Fear of your judgement causes them to put on their armour.

In the third-dimensional paradigm we are quick to condemn and criticize and the consequences are seen in personal and international relationships.

But as we see with fifth-dimensional eyes of love, we are aware of the hearts of others. There is nothing to hide for we can see their auras, where every emotion is revealed. We understand their hurt and their path of struggle, so we seek to support them with love and acceptance. When you approach someone's inner castle with respect, acceptance and love, they will feel safe and let you in.

The new spirituality will be that of the healed and open heart. Everyone will be friends. Then we will all connect with the cosmic heart. The result will be inner peace, international peace and intergalactic peace.

~ *Will Religion be a Thing of the Past?* ~

No, the beautiful loving essence of each religion will remain but the dogma surrounding it will dissolve. The glue that holds the cosmos together is love and this is the basis of spirituality. We can look forward to a world where there is spirituality within communities and between communities. It sometimes seems that we humans are the only ones who do not fully understand this already.

~ *Elemental Love* ~

Just as I was finishing this book I went for a walk round my local woods. I paused to admire a birch tree and to see if there were any elementals there.

One came jumping down from the tree. He was about four foot tall, green and thin and walked jauntily beside me. I must say at this point I assumed he was a pixie.

I telepathically asked him what he did for humans and he threw his arms wide, expanded his heart which glowed with light in an incredible way, and replied, 'Everything.'

When I wondered how his kind related to the other elementals in the wood, he looked at me sideways and answered, 'We are one – and we are different.'

So how do you see humans?' I persisted. Again he looked at me as if surprised by the question and said, 'We are one – and we are different.'

He walked with me out of the woods and along the road un-

*til he wanted to turn back. I called after him (telepathically).
'What's your name?' 'Gobolino,' he shouted back and laughed.
'I'm a goblin.'*

*I could not get the strange conversation or the love coming
from this elemental out of my mind. I also wondered about goblins as they have a bad reputation. Later I asked Kumeka who
told me that goblins are fifth-dimensional earth elementals that
have developed huge heart centres and a great capacity to love.*

For me that goblin summed up beautifully the spirituality of the future.

EXERCISE: *Open your Heart Centre*

Wherever you are, whether it is out walking, in the car, gardening or doing housework, open your heart centre. Imagine it glowing with light. Then
send threads of light to everyone and everything until all is linked with love.

EXERCISE: *Visualization to Practice Unconditional Love*

1. Find a place where you can be quiet.
2. Light a candle if possible.
3. Close your eyes and breathe comfortably until you feel really
    relaxed.
4. Picture a tall beautiful mountain in front of you, the top covered in
    snow.
5. Your guardian angel is with you holding your hand.
6. He leads you lightly and easily to the very top of the mountain. Here
    you are surrounded by angels singing of love and joy. There is only
    peace and acceptance.
7. From here you can see down the mountain all the peoples of the
    world. Notice how they are held back by dogma, ego and fear. How
    far do they reach up the slopes?
8. Send unconditional love down to all of them, welcoming them to
    come higher into Oneness.
9. Watch what happens as they are bathed in the pure light of One-
    ness.
10. Ask the angels to help them understand and give thanks for this.
11. Then open your eyes and return to the room.

CHAPTER 38

Enlightenment

Enlightenment is a state of being in which the consciousness expands to include all that is, so you become all-seeing and all-knowing. The energies coming into the planet at the cosmic moments of 11th November 2011 and 21st December 2012 offer huge opportunities for full or partial enlightenment.

There are also other opportunities during the following twenty years when the cosmic energies will assist everyone in their enlightenment journey. You are invited to take advantage of these special times.

When priestesses of Atlantis performed the dance of the seven veils they were symbolically describing the drawing back of these veils from the third eye. The dance was performed in honour of the divine feminine. When Atlantis collapsed the knowledge was taken to Egypt and Greece where lack of spiritual understanding gradually debased it into an expression of sexual allurement.

When someone is fully enlightened they transcend the lower limitations so, for example they can heal themselves if they desire to do so at a soul level. They can control their body functions and master their environment and circumstances. Most important they live in the moment, without anger about the past or fear about their future. There is no blame, just a knowing that all is well in the divine plan.

In contrast, ascension is a state of doing, of actively drawing down more of the light of the soul and Monad into the physical body. This raises the consciousness, expands spiritual awareness and can enable physical changes to take place. Enlightenment and ascension can take place at the same time though very often enlightenment comes first.

If you suddenly receive a flash of illumination about something, you move forward in your understanding. At that moment you have a spurt of spiritual growth and expand your level of enlightenment.

~ The Third Eye ~

The third eye is known as the all-seeing, all-knowing eye. In fact not everyone is clairvoyant even when they are fully enlightened, even though they 'know'. The journey to enlightenment is the removal of the seven veils of illusion.

The first veil to be dissolved is the seventh veil, the furthest from the third eye. However, you can thin the others before they finally release, so that they fade easily, without trauma or a difficult initiation. They can more easily be removed during moments of cosmic light or in special meditations. Alternatively you may wake up one morning feeling that things are different. You are seeing the world with new eyes. In that case a veil may have been released during your spiritual journey of the night.

Although enlightenment is a function of the third eye, you may have a blockage in another chakra which affects your third eye, for everything is connected.

The Seven Veils of Illusion

~ The Seventh Veil ~

This is the veil furthest from the third eye and the first to dissolve. When you awaken to your soul and recognize that you are responsible for your own individual journey, the seventh veil, which is red, dissolves. This happens when you finally let go of all victim consciousness and stop blaming or projecting onto others. This is the stage at which you take mastery of your life and, instead of saying, 'Poor me. I am so unlucky,' you ask yourself why you drew the circumstance or event into your life and you start to work on yourself to change your inner. As soon as you transform yourself, your outer conditions must reflect this and your life becomes more satisfactory.

~ The Sixth Veil ~

Many people in the world do not realize that there are other dimensions interwoven with ours. They only accept what they can see, hear and feel. The sixth veil, which is yellow, dissolves when you accept that there is a world beyond the physical. You realize that there are amongst us spirits of those who have passed, as well as angels, fairies and other beings. In order to remove this veil you must also believe in the spirit world and trust it. You must know deep within you that the other realms are able and willing to help you.

~ The Fifth Veil ~

This veil, which is pink, only dissolves when you hold unconditional love in your heart centre for everyone. There are often initiations involved with the removal of this veil for deep forgiveness of all those who have ever hurt you is necessary. Furthermore you must see the entire world and all the perpetrators of iniquity with eyes of love. You must be prepared to offer prayers for those who have been harmed as well as those who have inflicted harm on them, for you recognize that all is in agreement at a higher level. It involves seeing with divine eyes.

~ The Fourth Veil ~

This blue veil is released when you honour, respect and work with animals, nature and the elemental kingdom. This does not mean that you physically have to look after domestic or other animals but it does involve truly understanding that each animal is here on Earth to experience and learn just as we are.

Every animal has a soul, while some are part of a group soul and they are all on their own journey of enlightenment and ascension. Some, such as dogs, have incarnated to be companions and friends to humans. Our part of the agreement is to look after, honour and care for them. Other animals, such as domestic cats and the big cats, have incarnated to protect humans and the planet psychically from entities and negative energies that can harm us. Those creatures that we eat or hunt came in to experience life in the third dimension, not to be eaten or hunted by humans.

We are asked to talk to the spirits of the animals in meditation and honour them. You can also tell your spirit to go at night and talk to people about animals, for example your spirit can talk to the spirits of farmers who intensively farm chickens or any other animals about their higher purpose. This will eventually filter into their consciousness.

For the release of this veil, we must also recognize that nature is incredibly powerful, loving and responsive. We say that those to whom plants respond have green thumbs. In fact they empathize with nature, which rewards them with abundance.

Flowers radiate high frequency light. When someone has died we send flowers to the funeral as the angels can take their essence to help the spirit of the person who has died. The angels can also use their essence to help those who are mourning. The light carried by the flowers can heal those who are sick or unhappy if properly directed.

It is most important that we work with nature. The Universal Angel in charge of nature is Purlimiek, who radiates a wonderful soft green-blue colour.

There are many elementals and nature spirits, who have a role in the workings of nature, for example fairies look after flowers, elves help trees and pixies work with the soil. Many but not all of these spirits are made up of only one element, earth, air, fire or water. For the dissolving of the fourth veil of illusion we need to understand the benefits of working with the elementals, we can for example ask the elementals to help plants grow.

When slugs and snails were eating my newly planted peas I wanted to put slug pellets down. Kumeka was not impressed. He asked me to talk to the creatures but I said I had already done that and they did not listen. So he suggested I asked the elementals to work with the slug kingdom by talking to them about eating other things, for example to offer an area of plants to the slugs and snails. He said that some plants offer themselves as a sacrifice and through this they grow. He told me to plant the seedling, bless it and care for it and ask the elementals to look after it for the highest good. I did this and my vegetable garden flourished.

We can also ask the elementals to talk to those who are mistreating animals about their higher purpose.

~ The Third Veil ~

This veil, which is deep blue, automatically dissolves when you link with the angelic kingdom and similar beings from other planets, such as Kumeka, my guide or Fekorm, the Master of Music. Walk amongst them and live your life with them, so that they are an integral part of your life.

~ *The Second Veil* ~

This violet-coloured veil dissolves when you achieve universal consciousness. This happens when you are able to see into the cosmos and understand that all is connected, trees, stars, animals, rocks – everything. You must be able to see this with your mind's eye.

Once you fully understand the universal Metatron cube, which describes the interconnection of all, you are asked to hold it up so that it aligns with the planets concerned and let it work in our consciousness.

This is the last veil to be removed while you are in a physical body and when it has dissolved you are fully enlightened.

~ *The First Veil* ~

This is the closest veil to the third eye and is crystal clear. It is the last one to be removed, and this takes place after you have passed over, if you are ready. When this one is cleared you are in heaven or in the seventh dimension. When you live your life as an enlightened being this veil will dissolve when you die. Even then you may be tested. Kumeka gave as an example that you might be asked to undertake another incarnation! If you resist, your first veil does not dissolve.

While still in a body you can experience moments of being in this heavenly dimension, when this veil becomes thin.

> *I woke up on the morning of the funeral of my favourite aunt, Gwendy, expecting to feel miserable. But I was glowing. I literally felt as if gold light was pouring out of me. It obviously showed for a man who described me as luminous. Another person gasped when we talked and said, 'My God. You're glowing!'*
>
> *My aunt's spirit simply was not at her funeral. No one had any sense of her. Kumeka said that she had left Earth the moment she vacated her body and that Archangel Azriel, the angel of death, overlit me on the day of her funeral to show other people through me that there was life beyond death. It was a seventh-dimensional experience.*

~ How to Attain Enlightenment ~

The most important thing is to live your life with pure intent, fully engaging in every moment. You cannot be enlightened if you are ungrounded and not actually here. Watch your thoughts and words and see the divine in everyone.

All spiritual disciplines will assist your journey if performed with intention and focus. These may be prayer, meditation, invocations, affirmations, decrees, chanting mantras, yoga, silent contemplation or others of your choice. Certain energies like the Gold and Silver Violet Flame, the Gold Ray of Christ or the Mahatma, if used regularly can accelerate your journey. Visualizations are one of the big keys to transformation. Visualize your heart opening, your path being golden or whatever you need for your aspiration.

~ How Unicorns Help your Enlightenment ~

The unicorns are such enlightened beings that, if your heart is open, looking at a unicorn Orb will automatically remove the next veil to your third eye. The unicorns then agree to stay with you and help you remove all the remaining veils until the second one is dissolved, the last one to be dissolved while you are still in your physical body.

Archangel Azariel is helping the unicorns with this undertaking. Please do the following visualization with reverence and meaning.

EXERCISE: *Unicorn Visualization to Dissolve the Veils*

1. Open your arms to the world.
2. Remind yourself that you are an amazing divine being.
3. Make the sound 'maaah' three times with the intention of opening your heart.
4. Look at a unicorn Orb. *(see page 184).*
5. Imagine a magnificent white unicorn standing in front of you. Let the light from its horn touch your third eye. Visualize the next veil being pulled back like a curtain.
6. Thank the unicorn for coming to you and for working with you to dissolve the veils until you reach full enlightenment.

~ For Enlightenment with the Opposite Sex ~

If you are a woman and want to be enlightened with men, appreciate the energies they bring. Accept their essence and see their souls. Similarly if you are a man, do this with women.

EXERCISE: *Visualization to see the Essence of the Opposite Sex*

1. Find a place where you can be comfortable and undisturbed.
2. Light a candle to your intention to find enlightenment with the opposite sex.
3. With enlightened eyes see someone in front of you.
4. Appreciate their energies, their qualities.
5. Connect with their inner child. To do this, imagine them as a vulnerable three-year-old. Sense their innocence and their fears. Open your heart to their child and give them the love and acceptance they need.
6. Look for the light of their essence and honour it.
7. Glimpse the colours of their soul, their mighty higher self that is all loving.
8. Thank them for enlightening you.
9. When you open you eyes, notice how you feel.

~ For the Second Veil ~

Visualize light connecting everything, stars and planet, trees and plants, rocks and pebbles, people, animals, fish and insects.

EXERCISE: *Visualization to See the Connection in Everything*

Sit or lie on the grass on a clear starry night and visualize the links throughout the cosmos, then see that light connecting every single thing and person on Earth.

It is expected that over 70% of the people on the planet will be enlightened by 2032.

CHAPTER 39

Abundance and Manifestation

Abundance is about flowing with love and happiness, success and prosperity, knowing it will always flow in your life and that as a beloved child of the universe, you deserve it.

Because of their need to control, religions have historically promoted lack of self-worth, which impoverishes the spirit and results in poverty consciousness and belief in lack. Spiritual people know we live in an abundant universe, where there is enough for everyone. By 2032 the higher frequency of abundance consciousness will have consumed the lower fears.

~ The Keys to Abundance and Manifestation ~

1. **The power of asking**
   Angels are always with you, helping you, creating synchronicities, opening doors and whispering the best way forward but you must ask. They cannot contravene your free will by bringing you things you do not ask for.

2. **Manifestation at the third dimension**
   When you focus on something without doubt or deviation it must come about. You are activating the Spiritual Law of Manifestation but if it is not for the highest good, you are creating karma, as it is not for the benefit of the planet. In the third-dimensional world people have been focusing on their wants, not their needs. This means that you use your third eye mentally by focusing on desires rather than spiritually, for the highest good. This blocks it, holding back your enlightenment and ascension. This has not been a problem until recently because few people understood the power

of manifesting in this way. Now however, as a result of third-dimensional books on manifestation being published, many are doing it to such an extent that it is now holding back the progress of the planet. Ask for the highest good and then ask Michael to cut any cords. If you do ask for something for the highest good then the angels are delighted to bring it to you or something better.

3. **Manifestation at the fifth dimension**
   In the fifth dimension you are only interested in serving All That Is. So your requests are of this caliber. You are happy to let it go if it is not for the greatest benefit of all. At the level of this clear stream of consciousness all manifestations are for the benefit of all. Then your focus reaps prosperity and abundance of all kinds in a divine right way. When you do this there is no karma.

4. **Detach from or rise above collective unconscious beliefs**
   Beliefs held in the collective unconscious are like a grey cloud filled with sticky cobwebs enmeshing everyone at the third dimension. Individuals, families, communities and countries get so entangled that they cannot see the divine light or even a higher perspective. They all see the same lower reality. The collective is filled with anger, guilt, lack of trust and fears. The biggest is financial fear of lack and an inability to trust that the universe will support you.

   In order to be ready for the new Golden Age it is time to cut away any cords into the collective and place them in the light of Archangel Raphael, the angel of abundance, or into the fifth-dimensional consciousness.

5. **Embracing abundance, prosperity and love**
   Visualize what you do want and do not worry about what you do not want. Resistance blocks abundance.

   I was talking to a woman who hated her boss and could not say a good word about him. She kept being passed over for promotion even though she was efficient at her work. I suggested to her that she was blocking her good. She did not understand the power of her thoughts but I explained that they were energetically resisting her boss, who naturally withdrew from her. I asked her to visualize welcoming him into the office but she only reluctantly tried to do this and a week later there was no progress. She loved unicorns and suddenly she came up with the idea of visualizing him coming into work riding on one. This she could do. Every day she faithfully pictured him arriving into the room. She saw herself smiling and presenting him with flowers. It worked like magic. Her energy changed towards him and within two weeks he gave her a promotion.

So quit resistance and keep focusing on what you do want.

6. **Clarity about your next step, purpose or intention**
   If you want to bring something into your life it is important to be clear what it is. If you are not sure, sit down quietly and ask Archangel Gabriel to help you find what it is. You can ask that your spirit visit his Archangel retreat at Mount Shasta, California, during your sleep state if you wish to, stating that you desire clarity. You may need to do this for some time but when you have it, you can move ahead with confidence.

7. **Aligning to your soul energy**
   If you want to be a cook but you are working in an office, you are not abundant because you are not aligned to your highest truth. When you are abundant you are doing work which brings you joy. The reason world economies are collapsing is because the planet is moving up a gear spiritually and the cogs have to be in synch. So the economies of the world, banks, financial institutions and big business must move at faster frequency to allow this to happen. Currently they are not serving the highest good.

8. **Affirm that you deserve abundance**
   The moment you believe you deserve it, your vibration will automatically attract the abundance to you. If you receive something but deep inside you do not believe you deserve it, it will flow out of your life again. So keep affirming that you deserve.

9. **Enlightenment**
   Enlightenment is the true way to abundance. As the veils of illusion draw back from your third eye, you have clarity and the ability to focus. Your frequency is of the fifth dimension and you can manifest your own higher reality. The keys to enlightenment are in Chapter 37.

EXERCISE: *Visualization to Invoke Abundance*

1. Find somewhere you can be relaxed and quiet.
2. Invoke Archangel Gabriel. When you feel his white light around you, mentally ask for purification and clarity. Sit for a few moments while you accept light from him.
3. Ahead of you is a magnificent spiritual mountain. Notice what is holding you back. Guilt, fear, anger may be like grey balls attached to you or something else may be holding you back.
4. Cut those grey balls and transmute them in the Gold and Silver Violet Flame.
5. As you climb effortlessly up the mountain, you are entering the dark cloud of the collective unconscious. Be aware of the sticky cobweb enveloping you. There are many people trapped here with you.
6. Ask Archangel Michael to cut away the sticky strands. When he does so you can finally jump free.
7. Archangel Gabriel is taking you to a beautiful thundering white waterfall for purification. Let it cascade over you and wash you clean.
8. Now the clouds have rolled back and you can see the top of the mountain. The sun is pouring down.
9. A golden sun drenched path lies ahead of you. Visualize yourself and many others all walking up the golden path holding hands.
10. At the brow of the hill many angels are waiting. You are in the fifth dimension and all is light. Visualize what you want for the highest good.
11 Thank the archangels for their help. Then slowly come back into this world and open your eyes, taking the energy of abundance with you.

EXERCISE: *To Manifest Abundance*

1. Decide what you would like to manifest for the highest good.
2. Talk to someone else or if you have no one to talk to, find a quiet place and do this alone, speaking aloud.
3. Imagine it is now six months ahead. Name the month to focus yourself.
4. Imagine everything you asked for has come about. It is already in physical reality.

5. Talk with enthusiasm as if it is six month's time and your wish has already manifested. This helps to match your vibration with the vibration of that which you want.

EXERCISE: *Manifest Abundance with a Balloon*

1. Draw a balloon in gold, blue or pink with a string hanging down.
2. Inside it write down what you want to manifest.
3. Write underneath it. 'This or something better now manifests for the highest good of all.'
4. Draw a big pair of blue scissors cutting the string. The blue represents Archangel Michael, who is cutting your attachment to your manifestation.
5. Imagine your balloon flying up in the air and the angels taking it to the higher realms.

There is an abundance balloon on my website **www.dianacooper.com** which you can send to a friend or loved one. They are very powerful and I have seen angels and unicorns taking these balloons up to gather energy.

CHAPTER 40

The Importance
of Numbers

AT THE TIME OF GOLDEN ATLANTIS Archangel Metatron accessed from Source the science of numbers. He taught humanity that each number has a powerful cosmic influence.

Numbers are cosmic energies. Each one carries a unique vibration, which affects you when you connect with it.

For example the number 9 is an energy ball, which holds a frequency allowing endings or completions to take place. So if you live in a house of that number, you are automatically attuned to the broadcasting station of 9. The general influence on your life while you live there will be about tying up loose ends, possibly healing relationships, or even cleaning past lives without being aware you are doing so. You may experience the contentment which precedes a new seek and search.

If your home is number 28 the two digits are added together. 2 + 8 = 10. Then the 10 is reduced again 1 + 0 = 1. You home then is influenced by the cosmic number 1, the number of new beginnings or being individual and unique.

Dates of birth follow the same principle, which is why your date of birth was so carefully chosen by your soul and overlighting archangel before you incarnated. You will be tuned into one of the cosmic numbers and affected by its vibration throughout your life. For example someone born on 21.03.1950, the numbers will be added like this 2 + 1 + 0 + 3 + 1 + 9 + 5 + 0 = 21. 2 + 1 = 3. They will be in the influence of the cosmic vibration of 3.

The letters of your name are connected to a number, so what you are called profoundly affects you. Your parents, usually your mother, received your name from your soul before you were born and this is so important that the wrong name is hardly ever chosen.

~ *Influence of Basic Numbers* ~

1   This number influences you to make new beginnings or it could help you to become an Alpha, the first or very individual or unique.

2   This influences you to work in co-operation with others or do things in pairs, or seek a soul mate.

3   This is a very spiritual number influencing you with the energy of the Trinity. It helps to keep you stable so that you can ground yourself and reach up to spirit.

4   This number has a solid influence. It suggests you will build your dreams and hopes on a strong foundation, or seek justice and be practical.

5   This number vibrates at a level of wisdom and may enable you to be visionary. It assists to seek expansion during a lifetime.

6   This number brings an influence of sociability and at the highest level to seek spiritual community and unconditional love.

7   This number influences you to be a thinker, logical but at the same time to open up to the spiritual knowledge of the higher consciousness.

8   This is the number of infinity. It brings endless possibility and its highest influence is to create world transformation.

9   The influence of nine is calling you to your spiritual vision, enlightenment and divine wisdom. It helps you to complete your learning in a particular area.

Certain Master numbers are whole in themselves and the digits are not added up. These special numbers carry a powerful vibration and you are invited by the universe to notice and act on these numbers, for they hold a strong message for you. Your guides and angels have ensured that they come to your attention.

~ Master Numbers ~

11 This is the number of mastery and you are asked to examine the situations and relationships in your life. Take responsibility for having created them. Then you can change them if you wish to do so.

22 This is the number of the master builder, in other words it suggests it is time to co-create the life you want. So work positively to manifest your vision.

33 This is the number of the Christ consciousness, so if you see this number it is a message from the universe to work with the Christ light.

44 This is the vibration of Golden Atlantis and it invites you to bring forward the energy of Golden Atlantis into your life. Live as they did at that time in the fifth dimension, in harmony and co-operation with others, honouring and respecting all life forms.

55 This is the vibration of Metatron. It invites you to rise above worldly attitudes and work with Metatron for higher enlightenment. Remember that his colour is golden orange, so start to attune to him and listen to his messages.

66 Accept your role as a Being of the Universe. When you see this number you are reminded that you are not just a little personality on Earth. You are a great cosmic being and can influence the heavens.

77 This is the vibration of heaven. It invites you to live with your higher self in the Seventh Heaven, so it is calling you to spend as much time as possible connected to the Earth, the angels and masters as well as the cosmos. It is a call to higher enlightenment.

88 This is the vibration of your I AM Presence or Monad, which is your original divine spark from God. This number asks you to merge with the eternal love of your I AM Presence.

99 You have mastered the lessons of Earth.

When you see a number tripled it means the same as the double number but at a higher vibration. For example 333 invites you to work with the Christ consciousness but at a higher level.

While I was writing this a friend's partner was in hospital giving birth to their son. Andrew Brel, the then expectant father, is a musician. Their baby was born on 28th May 2009. Intuitively I added it up as $28 + 5 + 11$ it equals 44, the vibration of Golden Atlantis. When I told Andrew this he gasped. For the labour he had prepared a music playlist with dozens of classical albums. However his girlfriend kept requesting that he play the same album repeatedly. It was Andrew's own CD of 'Golden Atlantis' music, so Byron was literally born into the vibration of Golden Atlantis.

Then I realized that the 28 would usually be reduced, so that it would be added as $2 + 8 + 5 + 2 + 9 = 26 = 2 + 6 = 8$, the number of infinity with the possibility of helping to create world transformation. So I decided to consult my guide Kumeka who confirmed that Byron had been enormously light and powerful in Golden Atlantis and had incarnated to bring that energy forward for the world.

Perhaps he will be influenced by the number 8 during his childhood. Then as he grows into adulthood the sacred number 44 will gradually overlight him so that he can step into his true power and authority.

When Metatron started to connect with me I started for the first time to see just how many cars in my area had the number 55 on their registration plates. It was really quite strange, as I had simply never noticed before. Because of digital clocks and watches people's attention is being drawn to multiple numbers and some of these are extremely influential. In fact they are being used by spirit as mini wake-up calls from the universe and Kumeka gave me this information about them.

- **03.03** - things are going to start moving forward for you now.
- **04.04** - it is time to make a project solid, then fly with it.
- **06.06** - gather the help and co-operation you need around you.
- **07.07** - look at the higher spiritual perspective of what you are doing.
- **08.08** - trust the process and follow your guidance into the future.
- **09.09** - a phase is now ending.
- **10.10** - something new is starting so prepare for it.
- **11.11** - heralds new beginnings at a higher level. This number was set in the collective conscious aeons ago and it is at 11.11

that the new higher vibration will pour in at the cosmic moments.

- **12.12** - is the number of discipleship. It suggests you discipline yourself in a spiritual lifestyle.
- **13.13** - accept who you are and be a wise leader.
- **14.14** - prepare for the return of the Christ light.

If you see a number doubled, double the influence and energy. If you see it tripled, then multiply its effect by three.

Each star or planet has a cosmic number and they all work to create a tapestry of harmony. For example Earth is 3.

1. Sirius and Sun
2. Pleiades
3. Earth
4. Mercury
5. Mars and Andromeda
6. Milky Way, Venus and Jupiter
7. Orion and Andromeda
8. Neptune
9. Saturn and the Moon
   Note that Andromeda vibrates with 5 and 7.

By 2032 the true influencing potential of numbers will be recognized. It is time to start now to access more energy from the stars and planets themselves by honouring their numbers.

~ The Numbers with their corresponding Chakra, Location on the Planet, Galactic Connection and Archangel ~

No.	Chakra	Plantary Location	Galactic Connection	Archangel
1	Earth Star	London, UK	Sirius and the Sun	Sandalphon
2	Base	Gobi Desert, China	Pleiades	Gabriel
3	Sacral	Honolulu	Earth	Gabriel
3	Navel	Fiji	Earth	Gabriel
4	Solar Plexus	Whole of South Africa	Mercury	Uriel
5	Heart	Glastonbury	Andromeda and Mars	Chamuel
6	Cosmic Heart	Guatemala	Venus	
6	Throat	Luxor, Egypt	Milky Way	Michael
7	Third Eye	Afghanistan	Andromeda and Orion	Raphael
8	Embraces all chakras		Neptune	Azariel
9	Crown	Machu Picchu, Peru	Saturn and the Moon	Jophiel
10	Causal	Tibet	The spiritual aspect of Sirius	Christiel
11	Soul Star	Agra, India	Alcyon	Mariel
12	Stellar Gateway	Arctic	Linked to an energy cluster in the Pleiades, which connects to a wormhole that accesses Source	Metatron

Where I mention two galactic connections the first has more power, while the second has a lesser influence.

CHAPTER 41

Switches for Bringing
back the Energy of Atlantis
at a Higher Level

THE ENERGY OF ATLANTIS is latent inside our chakras. We need to fine-tune the centres so that we can access it and the angels and unicorns will help us to do this.

1. The first switch is that of enlightenment. The unicorns will assist every single person whose heart is open to dissolve the veils of illusion so that they can reach enlightenment. There is detailed information about this in Chapter 37.

2. Call the unicorns into your dreams for specific purposes. Ask them to work with your twelve chakras from the Earth Star upwards to bring them into a fifth-dimensional frequency AND ask the angels to sing the right tone for each of the chakras as they do this.

My friend and sound healer Diane Egby Edwards has extensively researched and experimented with sound, especially sound healing. She says that, while all sound is beautiful, the intervals are recognized to have a number of different psychological, emotional and physical effects. She has very generously allowed me to use this explanation from her *Magical Sound* CD:

'Everything that has matter has its own sound, for example each tree or every cell of your body which emits vibrational frequencies beyond our range of hearing.

A vibration is a wave and frequency is the speed of the wave. All beings and all matter is made of molecules, Each has its own vibrational frequency which either resonates or dissonates with every other molecule in that being. When all of our molecules resonate in harmony together there is well being. When there are dissonant molecules there is physical or psychological illness. When molecules are subjected to certain frequencies they vibrate sympathetically. That is the basis of sound healing.

Combinations of certain frequencies create sounds that are more powerfully healing than others. These combinations are called intervals. Each interval has a different special effect because of all the harmonics that are created, for example when sounding a C + G together, you don't just hear those fundamental notes. Those two are weaving a range of other notes into the sound you hear. The others are all sounds that resonate with the C + G and are called harmonics. It is these that do the healing so effectively. C + G, known as the perfect 5th, is the most perfect sound in the universe, which can take people into bliss.'

Diane has kindly given me the following notes, which she dowsed under the direction of Kumeka and Fekorm the Master of Music, for the angels of each of the chakras.

Third interval	=	happiness and joy
Fourth interval	=	strange, mystical
Fifth interval	=	aligns chakras, moves energy, expansion
Sixth interval	=	purity, love, sweetness

3. Ask the angels and unicorns to help you connect your heart to the hearts of animals.

4. Ask Archangel Sandalphon to place you in a fifth-dimensional bubble. See Chapter 32.

5. Ask the angels of love to place a bubble of love round you and round other people.

6. Each day ask the angels to help you to see, hear and speak in a fifth-dimensional way.

7. Many people are not really connected to Earth. They are simply here on it. You cannot be truly happy and help the planet to evolve unless you feel it. To help you do this here is an exercise you can practise.

~ The Twelve Chakras with their corresponding Archangels, Sounds and Colours ~

Chakra	Archangel	Notes to attune to chakra	Fifth-dimensional colour
Earth Star	Sandalphon	F + B (4th interval)	Black and white (yin yang)
Base	Gabriel	E + B (5th interval)	Platinum
Sacral	Gabriel	E + B (5th interval)	Pale pink
Navel	Gabriel	E + B (5th interval)	Orange
Solar Plexus	Uriel	D + B (6th interval)	Gold
Heart	Chamuel	F + C (5th interval)	White
Throat	Michael	D + A (5th interval)	Royal blue
Third Eye	Raphael	E + A (4th interval)	Crystal Clear
Crown	Jophiel	C + A (6th interval)	Crystal clear
Causal	Christiel	A + C (3rd interval)	White
Soul Star	Zadkiel and Mariel	C (512H) F C (128H)	Magenta
Stellar Gateway	Metatron	G + C#	Deep gold

EXERCISE: Connect with Archangel Sandalphon

a. Connect with Archangel Sandalphon. You may be outside with your feet on the earth or you may be indoors visualizing this.

b. Imagine roots going down from your feet through your Earth Star into the loving centre of the Earth.

c. Then bring the energy up to your heart, so that you feel loved and a sense of belonging.

   d.   Then you know that Mother Earth truly passionately loves you
      and you are able to respond from your heart. (Kumeka insisted
      on the words 'truly passionately' to emphasize the importance
      and depth of the love Lady Gaia has for each of us.)

8. Connect to the sun and bring in the divine masculine. Connect to
   moon and bring in the divine feminine… to do this consciously go
   outside and bathe in their light. Breathe the energy into your cells.

9. Honour the energy of the water, e.g. waves, waterfalls, rushing riv-
   ers… and at the same time honour a drop of water. A single drop of
   water on your tongue embodies the essence of life.

10. Open your twelve chakras, with your Earth Star connected to the
    Earth and your Stellar Gateway wide open to Source. Bring up
    Earth energy to your heart and bring down Source energy to your
    heart. Then radiate love and peace round the world from your
    heart.

11. Sit quietly and visualize that you are holding the whole planet in
    your cupped hands. Give it love and receive love from it.

CHAPTER 42

Our Roles
in the Plan

YOU ARE BLESSED to be on Earth at this time, with its amazing privilege of bringing in the energies of 2012 and then preparing for the new Golden Age. There has never been an opportunity for spiritual growth like this one and you are asked to make the most of this God-given chance.

In order to be prepared you are expected to clear yourself of all fear and negativity and replace it with love, peace, joy and abundance. You can do this by working with the exercises in this book. The more you transmute, the greater will be your Light and the more the angels and Illumined Ones can work through you.

~ How to Assist the Process ~

1. Bring your own life into peace and harmony. Your energy will then automatically lift the vibrations of everyone with whom you come into contact.

2. Recognize that everyone is equal and treat them as such.

3. Honour all life forms on the planet, from rocks, insects and plants to animals and humans.

4. Give no energy to fear, darkness or mass hysteria. Instead focus on the good, the wise and great, so that it expands.

5. Visualize everyone throughout the world living in peace and love.

6. Walk with your feet on the earth and your head in the heavens.

If enough individuals do these things, the consciousness of all must inevitably rise. Your task is to hold your light steady and act as a beacon, for you may find you are able to influence thousands of souls and even lead them into ascension.

~ *My Personal Preparations* ~

On a practical level I have made my home as ecological as possible with solar panels and wood burning stoves. I conserve water in every way I can. Because I believe in self-sufficiency I am growing vegetables and fruit and plan to expand this.

Metatron is ensuring that everyone is in the right place at the right time. In accordance with his guidance I am looking for somewhere where the land itself is pure, where I can co-create a fifth-dimensional community. I know this will happen in his timing, not mine!

In the meantime I am making my home as light and bright as possible, so I have had huge new windows put in wherever possible. This makes it easier for the house to hold the fifth-dimensional energy. Every day I ask Archangel Sandalphon's angels to stand by my gate and place anyone who enters in a fifth-dimensional bubble. There are also crystals by the gate and at the windows to ensure that anything or anyone of a lower frequency cannot enter.

Both Kumeka and Metatron keep reminding me that the spiritual worlds love fun and laughter, so I have built play things in the garden for my grandchildren and visiting children – to say nothing of adults. We all love the trampoline, the zip wire and swings but the entrance to the den is only big enough for little ones!

To maintain the highest frequency I connect with the trees in my garden and honour them. I also honour the elementals. Sometimes there are hundreds of them around my home. When my new baby granddaughter came to visit, they gathered to greet her and we paused to let them say hello to her. They were thrilled for it is not often they are introduced with love to a human baby!

With every decision I ask myself, 'What would be the highest thing to do here?' That is why I handed the Diana Cooper School to the teachers as a non-profit organization and we are co-creating something much better than I could have done on my own. It has been an amazing experience. In letting go I received more than I would ever have dreamed possible.

My biggest challenge is to balance work and leisure. It is far too easy for me to overwork. But I am being forced to listen! Kumeka buzzes my left ear and Metatron my right one when they are telling me to stop and relax.

Am I looking forward to the next twenty-five years? Absolutely yes. I think it is awesome to be part of this unimaginable change. I love the idea of creating a new way of living in as natural and sustainable a way as possible. Walking hand in hand with angels, masters, unicorns and elementals and allowing them to guide and assist me makes my heart sing.

Let us all bring joy and laughter into the world and move forward together into this new and wonderful way of life.

Orbs

IF YOU LOOK AT THESE ORBS of unicorns with your heart open, they will connect with you and help you dissolve the veils of illusion over your third eye. Then they will stay and work with you to release the remaining veils until you reach full enlightenment. See chapter 38 on Enlightenment for more inspiring information.

Bridget Breen

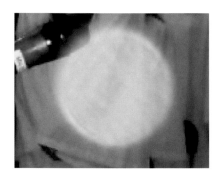

Tracy Fahey

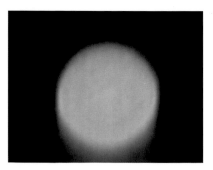

Stacey Lee Revoldt

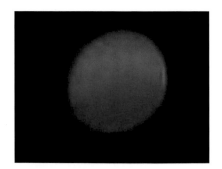

Michael & Ronnie Olivier

Bibliography

Cooper, Diana; *A New Light on Angels*,
Findhorn Press, 1996/2009.

Cooper, Diana; *The Wonder of Unicorns*,
Findhorn Press, 2008.

Cooper, Diana / Croswell, Kathy; *Enlightenment Through Orbs*
Findhorn Press, 2009.

Cooper, Diana / Croswell, Kathy; *Ascension Through Orbs*
Findhorn Press, 2009.

Cooper, Diana / Hutton, Shaaron; *Discover Atlantis*,
Hodder Mobius, 2006 / Findhorn Press, 2008.

Egby Edwards, Diane; *Magical Sound* CD 2009

Goldman, Jonathon; *Healing Sounds: The Power of Harmonics*,
Healing Arts Press, 1996

Haich, Elisabeth; *Initiation*,
Aurora Press, 1994/2000

Hamel, Peter Michael / Lemesurier, Peter; *Through Music to the Self*
Shaftsbury Element Books, 1986

Angels of Light Cards

BY

DIANA COOPER

Angels are waiting and happy to help you at all times. Under Spiritual Law they cannot step in until you ask. Whenever you have a problem, there is an angel standing by you, awaiting your permission to assist.

Angels cannot and will not help you if you ask for something from neediness and greed. Nor will they help you receive something which is not spiritually right. Recognize your authority and make your requests from wisdom and strength. You may also ask the angels to help someone else for his or her highest good, not necessarily for what you think that highest good might be. Your thoughts to that person create a rainbow bridge along which the angels can travel to help him or her.

You can also ask the angels to help the planet.

Each of the 52 Angel Cards included in this deck represent a different Angel quality, and can be used for guidance, inspiration and affirmation. The cards will help you tune in to the higher vibrations of the Angels, and allow you to feel the helping hands of these beings at all times. Following the inspiration of the Angels will raise your consciousness, which will automatically help you attract to yourself people and situations of a higher vibratory level and release old negative thought patterns. Carry these cards with you wherever you go and use them to remind yourself of the presence, guidance and help of the Angels in your life, always and everywhere. You are never alone or lost when the Angels are with you.

Set of 52 cards + 2 instructions cards
in desktop presentation stand with slipcase – ISBN 978-1-84409-141-6
***Pocket edition:** set of 52 cards + 2 instructions cards*
in tuckbox – ISBN 978-1-84409-171-3

A New Light on Angels

BY

Diana Cooper

Completely revised, updated and expanded edition of the bestselling *A Little Light on Angels* with new original colour illustrations by Damian Keenan

"I believe in angels" is the title of a well-known song – but do we really? With this book, we meet everyday folks who have experienced angels in their lives. Yes, angels do exist: they are highly evolved beings that have a lighter and faster vibration than humans, and are normally invisible to us. However, many of them have chosen to serve mankind and are available to help, support, heal and guide us – all we have to do is ask! There are small angels who care for the little daily tasks and enormous beings that overlight great universal projects. There are angels who can assist in healing and other who attend celebrations and rituals.

With close to 50% new materials including new stories, new visualizations and new information on Archangels, this edition of *A New Light on Angels* gives us guidance on how we can call on them for help and companionship in our lives. We are surrounded by angels, all we have to do is raise our consciousness to become aware of them and communicate with them, to welcome them into our lives and allow the joy, light and peace of their presence into our hearts.

"This whole matter of dealing with angels is far more business-like than the unitiated might think, and it is not just about peace, healing and a healthy aura. Angels can also be called upon to solve practical problems, and there is even an angel of parking spaces."
— RONALD WHITE, THE SUNDAY TIMES

144 pages paperback, full colour, illustrated
ISBN 978-1-84409-166-9

FINDHORN   PRESS

Life Changing Books

For a complete catalogue,
please contact:

Findhorn Press Ltd
117-121 High Street,
Forres IV36 1AB,
Scotland, UK

t +44 (0)1309 690582
f +44 (0)131 777 2711
e info@findhornpress.com

or consult our catalogue online
(with secure order facility) on
www.findhornpress.com

For information on the Findhorn Foundation:
www.findhorn.org